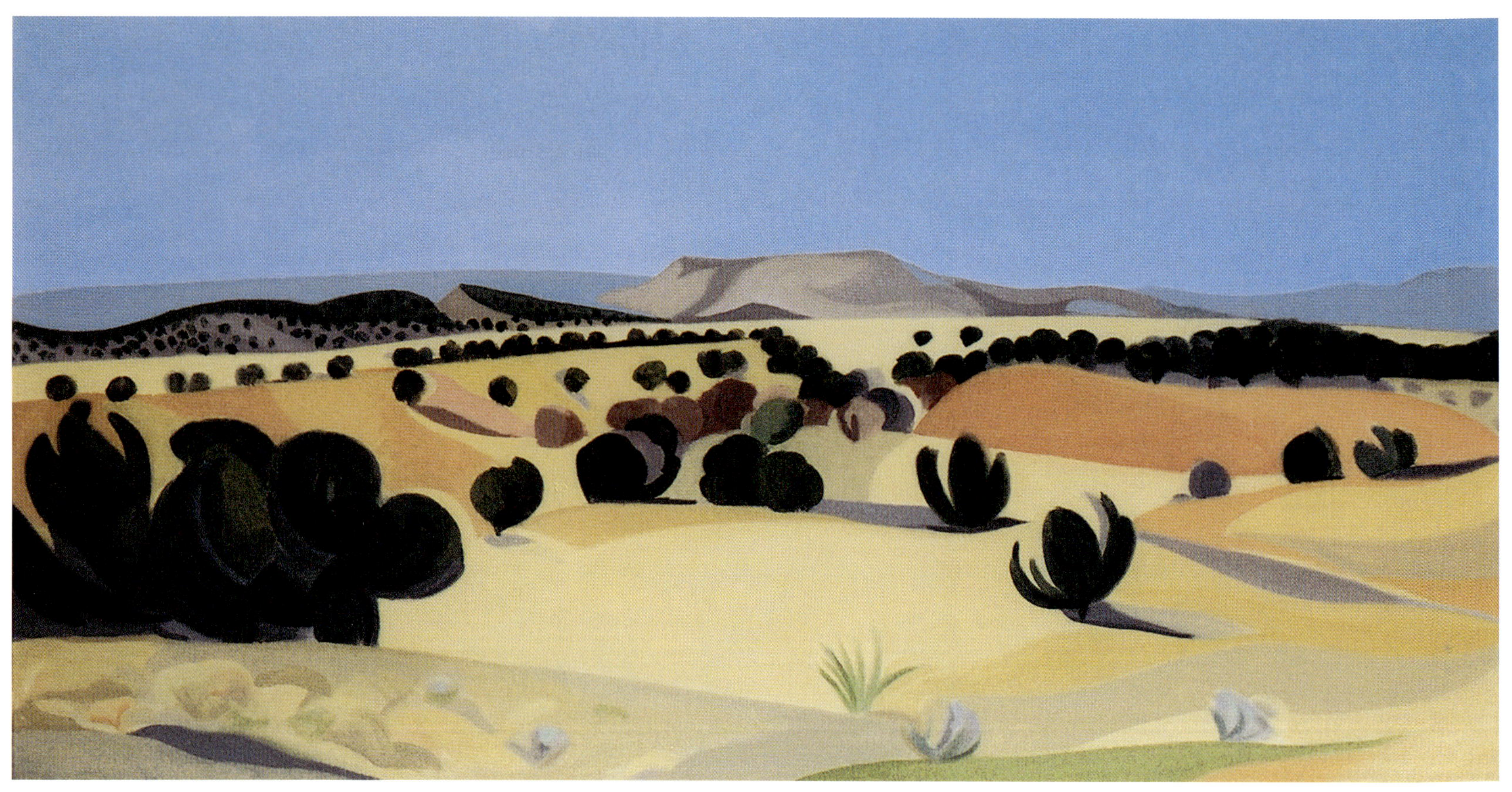

Piñons and Distant Mountains, 2002

oil on linen, 16" × 32"

JOEL GREENE

new mexico modernist

NEW MEXICO MAGAZINE ARTIST SERIES

Author: Gussie Fauntleroy

Executive Editor: Bette Brodsky

Editor: Ree Strange Sheck

Book Design & Production: Bette Brodsky

Publisher: Ethel Hess

Photography of Artwork: Joel Greene

Library of Congress Control Number: 2004100964

ISBN: 0-937206-81-4 (regular edition)
0-937206-82-2 (limited edition)

Cover: *Red Rocks Abiquiú*, 2003
Oil on board, 11" × 14"

Title page: *Red Hills Near Cundiyó*, 2001
Oil on board, 9" × 12"

Table of contents: *Rain Nine Mile Road*, 2002
Oil on board, 9" × 12"

Printed in China

We wish to thank:

Terry and David Peak, Logan, Utah
Patricia and Karl Jonietz, Santa Fe, N.M.
Debra Echt, Woodside, Calif.
Anne and Michael Brody, Chicago, Ill.
Ann and Miles Brasch, Bloomfield Hills, Mich.
Laurie Dawson, Jefferson City, Mo.
Peggy and Francis Reed, Castle Rock, Colo.
June Smith and Steve Pensinger, Boston, Mass.
Robert Bell, Santa Fe, N.M.
Bob and Pat Anker, Carmel, Ind.
Ernesto Mayans
Robert Redford

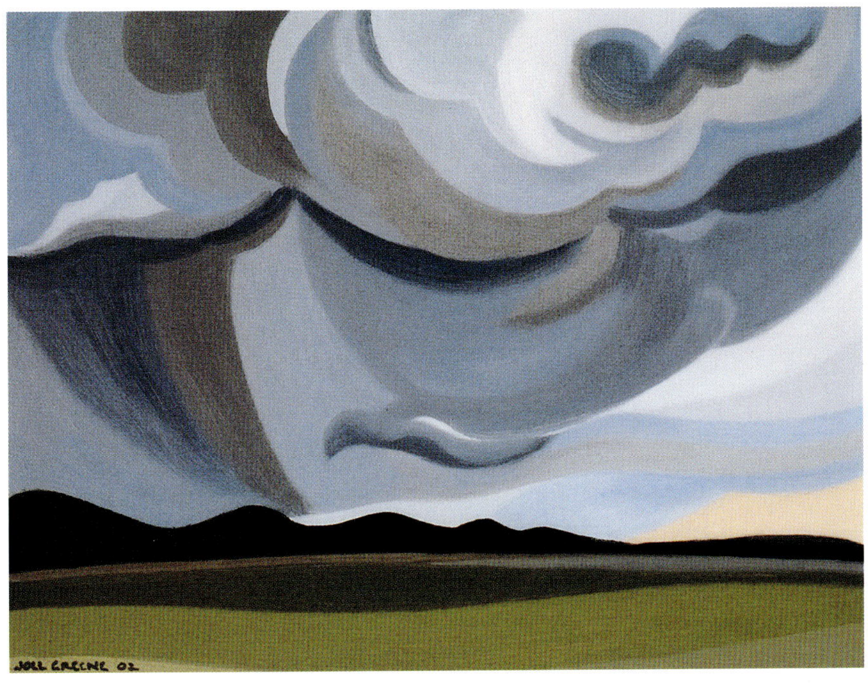

table of contents

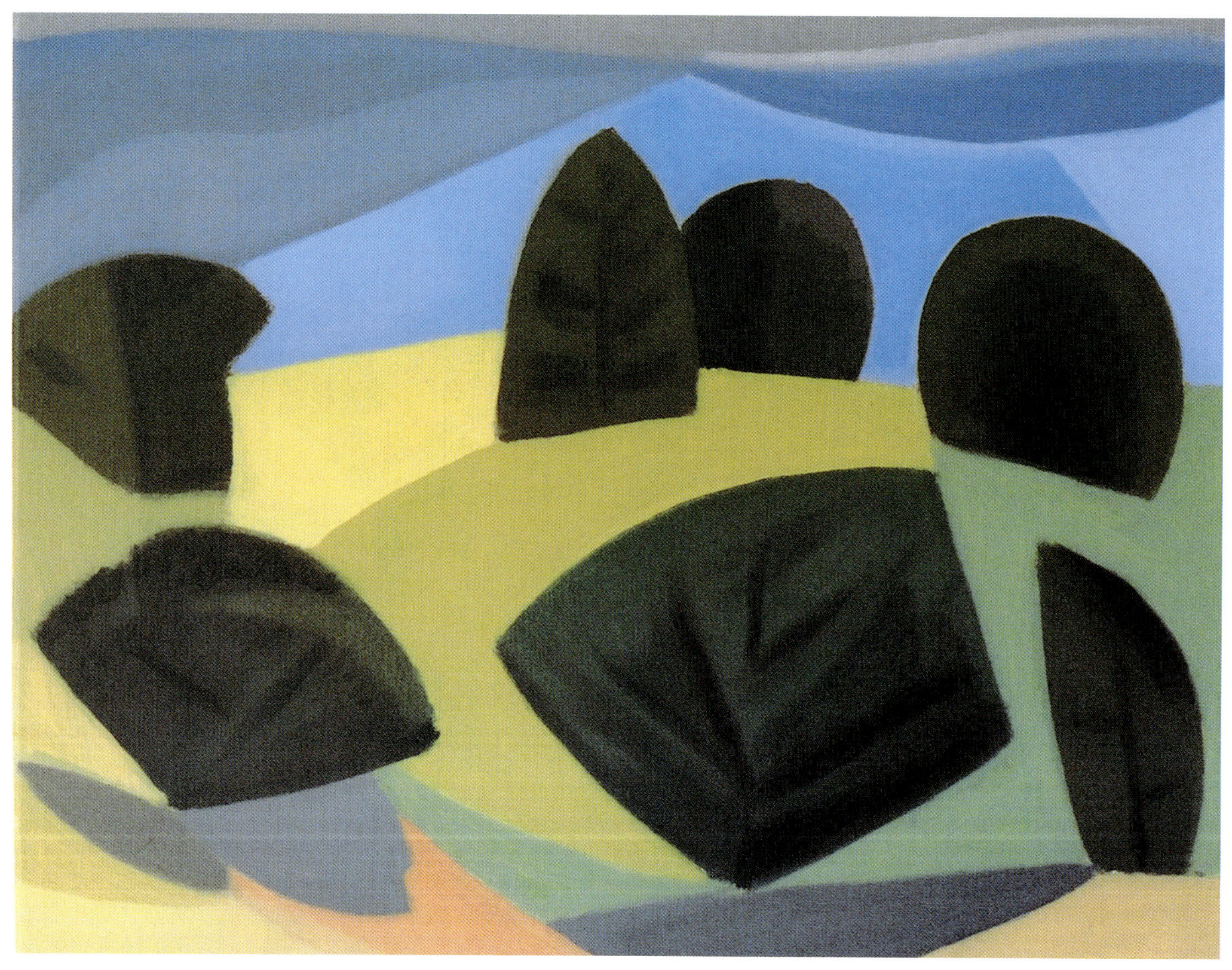

Yellow Hill With Piñon, 1996

Oil on board, 8" × 10 ½"

Joel Greene

pragmatism and passion

In 1971, when Joel Greene was finishing high school and considering his next step, his father wrote a letter to the Smithsonian Institution, which not long before had begun publishing its flagship magazine. The elder Greene approached the venerable organization for an opinion on which state universities and colleges had the best art departments. The move was a way of satisfying both father and son—the father wanting a practical, well-rounded education for his offspring and the son just interested in art. This approach reveals qualities that seem to have been passed down through the Greene family genes: an effective blend of imaginative spunk and methodical order, of pragmatism and passion.

Joel's great-uncle Ed, for example, was a nationally acclaimed opera singer and portrait painter who lived to be 105. He changed his surname to Molitore (his mother's maiden name), married a soprano in the courtyard of an Italian castle, painted portraits of corporate executives, and carried around a transistor radio constantly tuned to the San Francisco Stock Exchange. He also gave his grandnephew the young boy's first books on drawing, effectively striking a match that soon would blaze into an inextinguishable flame of love for art.

Joel possesses an equally diverse set of character traits, including an enormously educated mind and nimble curiosity, tucked behind a quiet-mannered facade. There's a subtle spirit of playfulness often marked by self-effacing humor. And there's stubborn devotion to daily routine: in the studio by 8 a.m., lunch at noon, an afternoon walk on the road near his studio in the foothills outside Santa Fe, a glass of wine at 4 p.m., and, before he gave up tobacco, a smoke on his pipe. Yet his paintings and prints reveal a man who perceives the world in complex and infinitely interchangeable combinations of swirling, flowing, passionately dancing patterns, colors and forms. He revels in the liberty—bequeathed by the Modernists whose living legacy he continues to amplify—to push color, compress space, bend imagery and shift angles in the service of his own vision. And it is a vision rooted in deep familiarity with the landscape of New Mexico.

Born in Denver, Joel grew up in Las Vegas, N.M., where his father taught psychology and behavioral science at New Mexico Highlands University. His mother, Frankie, was a pharmacist and homemaker who raised three children. During Joel's boyhood and in the decades afterward, she was a devoted supporter of his interest in art—an interest that grew more serious in high school, when he signed up for summer art classes at Highlands: the school's art department was headed by Elmer Schooley, who went on to become one of New Mexico's most renowned painters. At graduation, after considering the Smithsonian's suggestions, Joel settled on the University of Iowa, with its acclaimed printmaking department headed by Mauricio Lasansky. His years at Iowa included not only intense training but also wild artistic experimentation. He now looks back on that time with bemused amazement. "Jeez, I don't know how they let me graduate," he laughs. "Gosh, did I flounder around and have the goofiest ideas. I was looking for some vague, atmospheric stuff, I guess. Now I'm looking for a kind of crystal clarity in what I do."

Unfettered enthusiasm as a student may have kept him in the studio for 14 hours at a stretch, but Joel's methodical, studious approach to the process of printmaking resulted in his serving as a teaching assistant for two years. His master's thesis was the creation of a print-shop manual so complete and well organized that teaching assistants and students used it for years afterward. A decade after receiving his master's degree in fine art, he was invited to return to his alma mater to speak to the printmaking students about his life as an artist. It's a life, he acknowledges, that is richer for the Dostoevski he read and the interest in world history he cultivated through a well-rounded education—just as his father knew it would be.

At the same time, Joel's study of art history opened one particularly consequential window, into the world of Modernism, that would serve as the jumping off point for his artistic sensibilities from that time forward. The radical approach to organizing the picture plane and redefining representational painting introduced by Cubists Pablo Picasso and Georges Braque would resonate intensely with the young artist, whose own focus has always been on the formal elements of an image rather than its narrative traits. When he returned to his home state in 1981, Joel opened a private intaglio print shop, which he continues to run, assisting other artists in the creation of their own prints. He has been a full-time artist in Santa Fe since 1983, also designing and building all his own frames.

Through his paintings and prints Joel maintains what one admirer describes as a conversation, a lively exchange with the great Modernists of the past. With the New Mexico landscape permeating his experience, this dialogue echoes especially the artistic voices of New Mexico Modernists of the early 20th century, such as Andrew Dasburg, Jozef Bakos and Marsden Hartley. Yet Joel's contribution to the conversation is uniquely his own. As his work has evolved over the years, he has refined a visual vocabulary of swirling shapes and volumetric forms that seem to define the essence of this place and its topography, vegetation and weather, allowing the viewer to take part in the exchange in an ongoing way. As gallery owner Ernesto Mayans puts it, "In changing the reality of painting, Joel Greene is also changing our perception of reality."

See for yourself, especially if you happen to be in northern New Mexico: after absorbing Joel's imagery for a while, step outside. Look around at the junipers, the hills, the sky. Chances are they will transform before your eyes into the shapes and rhythms of Joel's work.

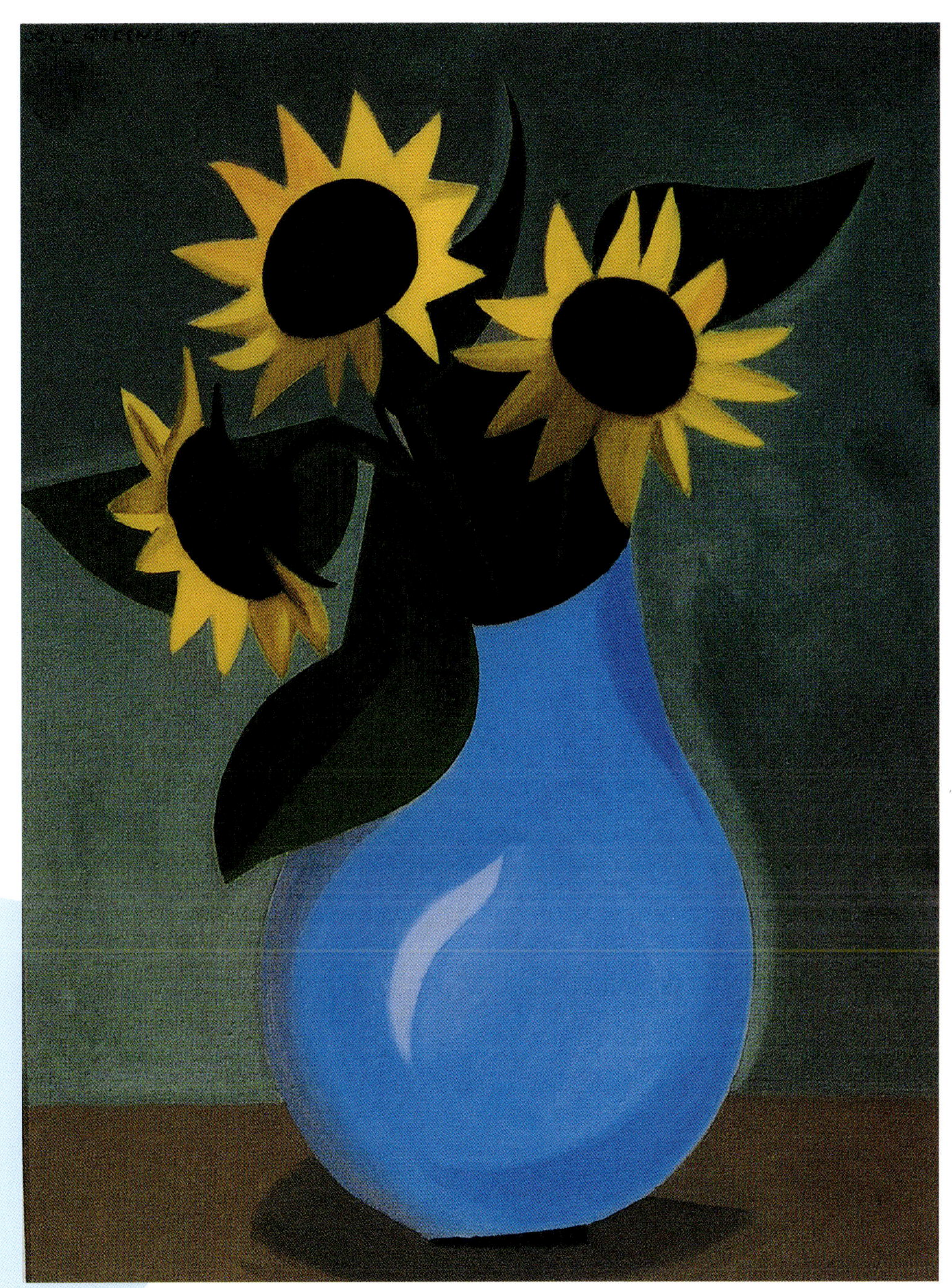

Sunflowers, 1997

Oil on board, 16" × 12"

Trees, Pond and House, 1988
Oil on board, 24" × 18"

explorations in the modern realm

All this is games and playing. —Joel Greene

As an art student at the University of Iowa, Joel was immersed in the world of printmaking, with its methodical process and the meticulous overlay of images in a multicolor etching or engraving. Perhaps for this reason, when he turned his attention to painting in the early 1980s, it was the "architecture of a painting," as he puts it, that captured his interest. Traditional representational painting, with its depth of visual perspective, realism in details and storytelling capacity, was fine for other artists. But Joel's creative senses were rocked, and still are, by the artistic freedom he inherited from the European and American Modernists of the late-19th and early-20th centuries, in particular the Cubists. It was a freedom—revolutionary in its time—to perceive an object or scene, dissolve it into constituent elements of color, perspective, movement, line and form, and put it back together in an entirely new and fresh way.

Working in his first Santa Fe studio on Early Street, Joel began what has become his modus operandi as an artist: serious play. After years of art-history study, both formal and on his own, he set his gaze on artists and periods that attracted him most. Then he turned to the canvas to see what would happen as he expressed his own world through the energy absorbed from earlier masters. The German Expressionists gave him vivid color, as in *Trees* (1984) and *Nudes in the Landscape* (1985). But it was Picasso and Braque who gave him permission to flatten the picture plane and rearrange objects to suit his sense of geometry, visual cadence and design.

Joel moved his studio in 1986 to an Upper Canyon Road compound known as the New School studios. Suddenly he was enveloped in a cottonwood-canopied ecosystem fed by mountain streams that soon was reflected in his art. In *Trees* (1986) and *Trees, Houses and Hills* (1986), for example, he created complex, formal images that lean heavily in the direction of abstraction yet never relinquish the artist's connection with the natural world. At the same time, his palette began to soften into a quiet and elegant subtlety that has characterized his use of color ever since. These early works marked the beginning of a long and continuing multidimensional conversation: between artist and subject, artist and canvas, artist and viewer, and the artist and his Modernist muses from the past.

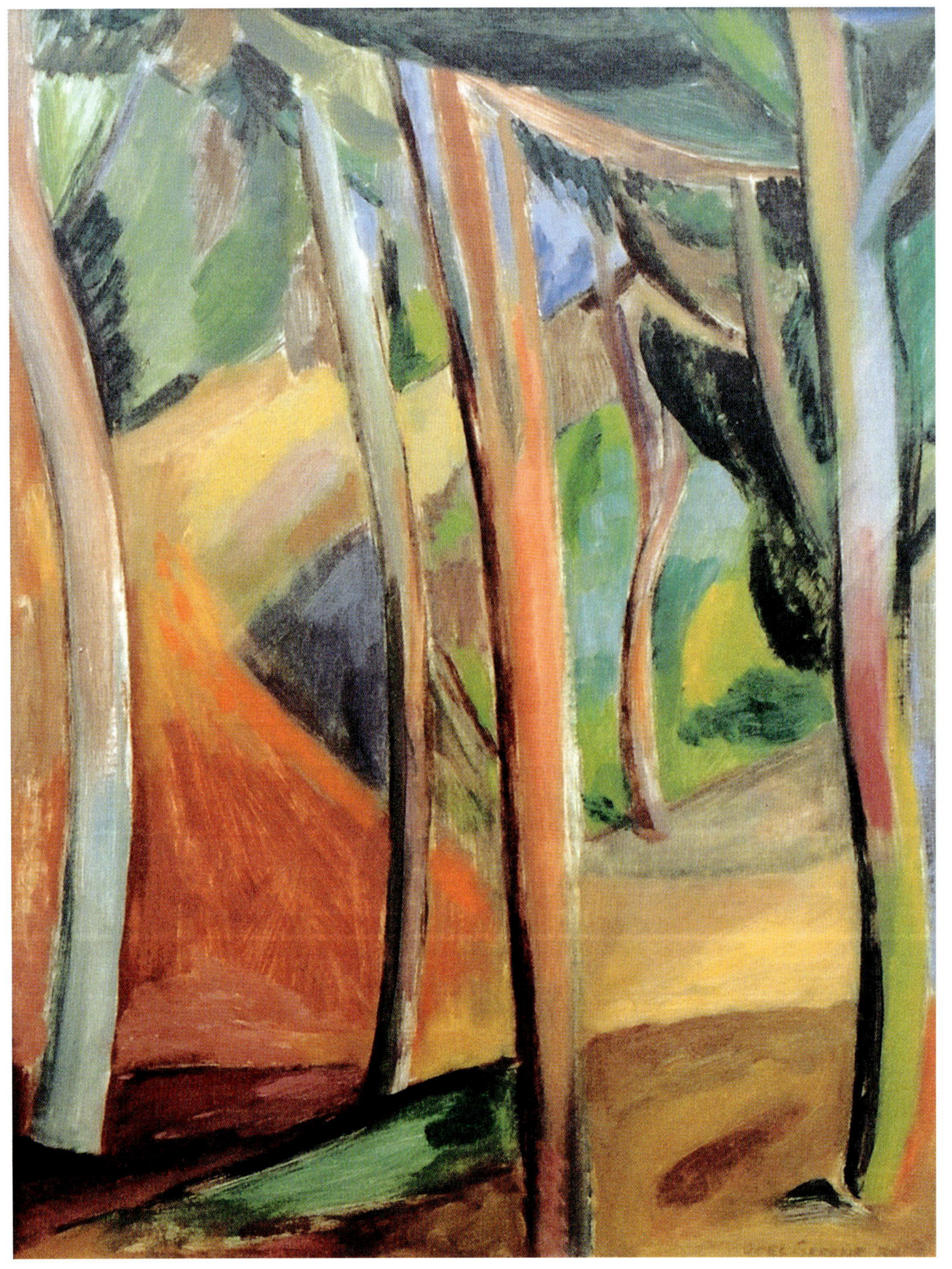

Trees, 1984
Oil on board, 17 ½" × 14"

Nudes in the Landscape, 1985
Oil on board, 16" × 12"

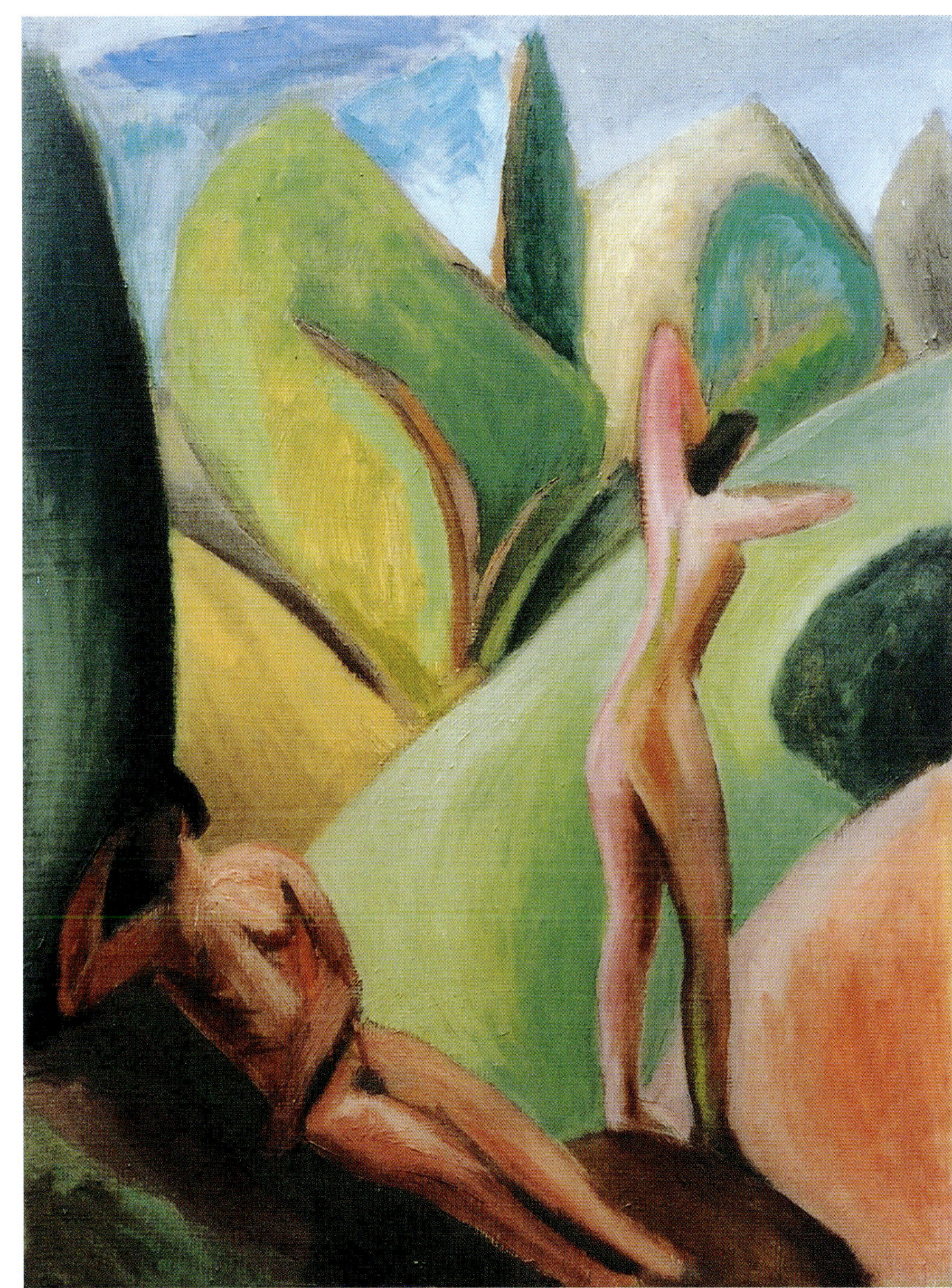

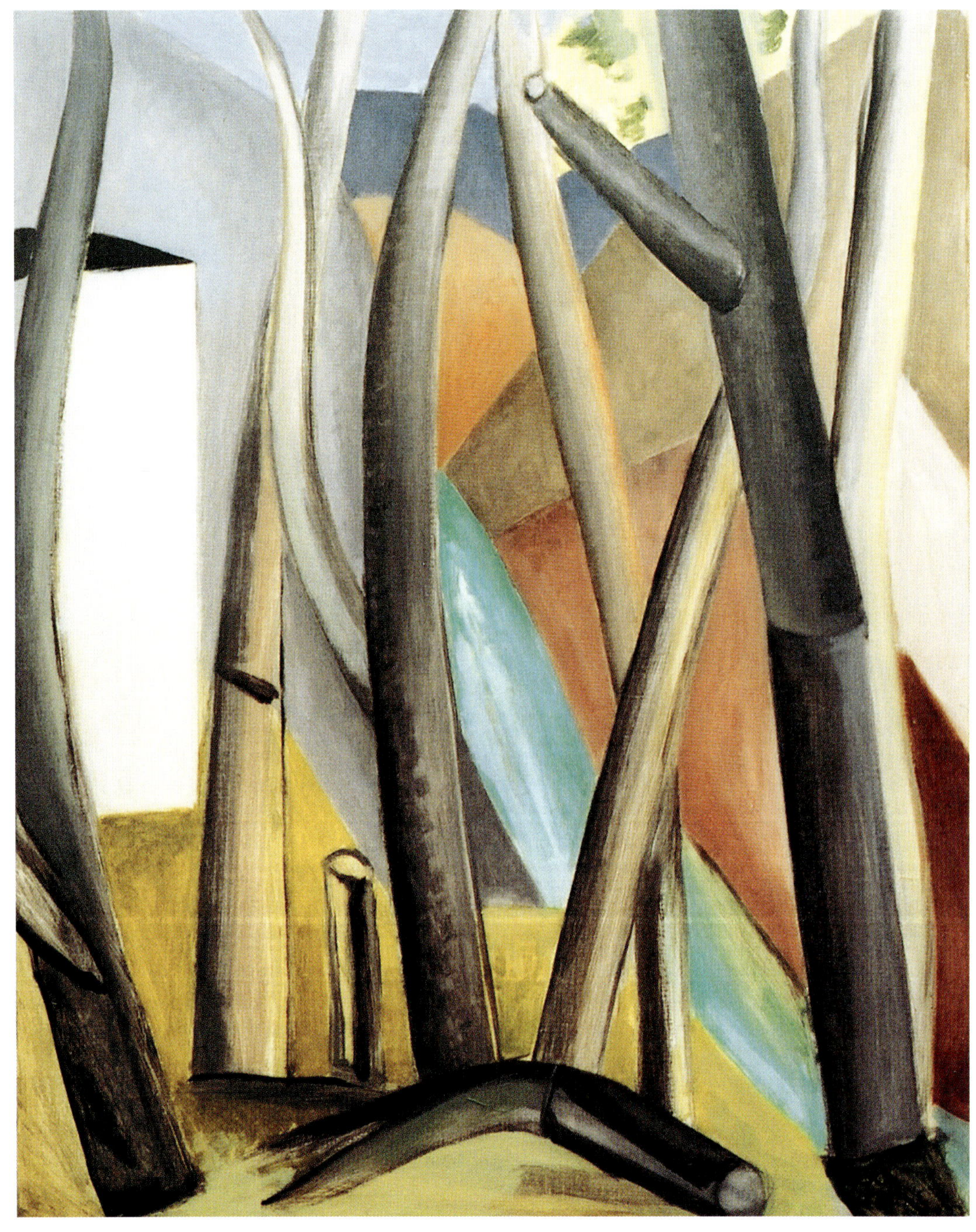

Trees, 1986
Oil on board, 20" × 16"

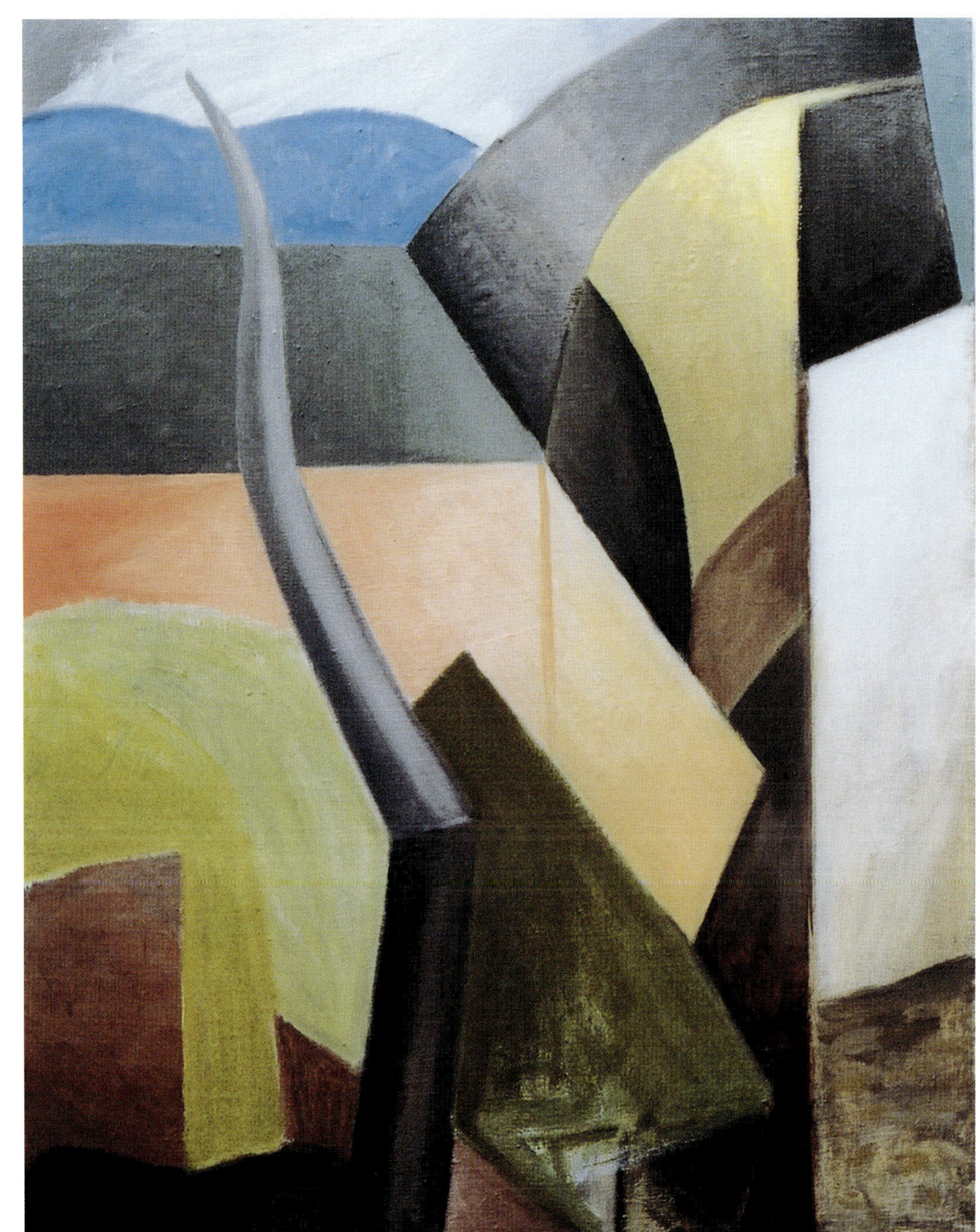

Trees, Houses and Hills, 1986
Oil on linen, 20" × 16"

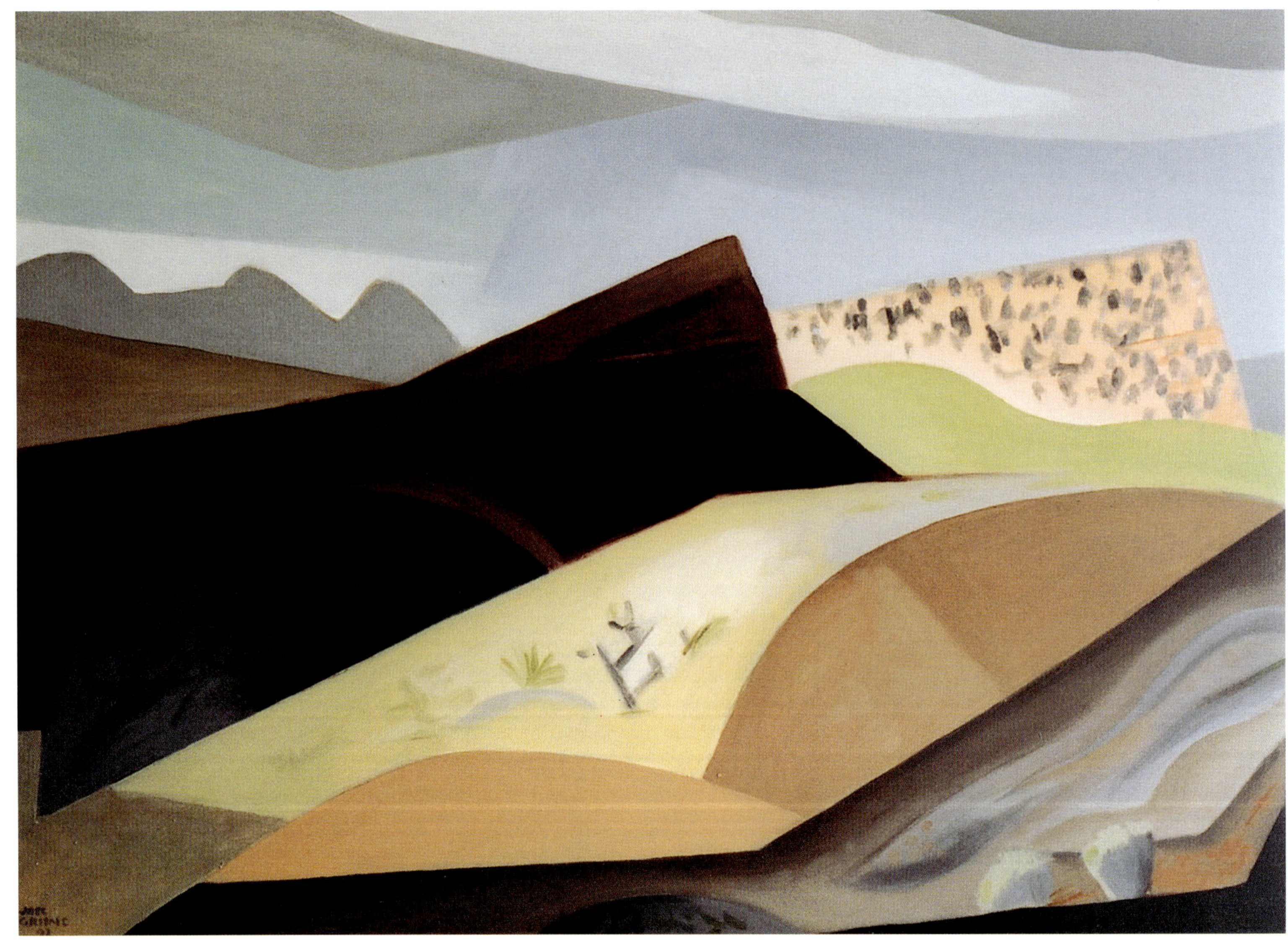

Arroyo and Mesa, 1992 Oil on board, 17" × 24"

the landscape: a vocabulary of forms

I'm such a country mouse. —Joel Greene, laughing

Joel moved to his current studio in 1989, and with the move came an opening into a new phase in his landscape imagery. The spacious printmaking and painting studio, on Nine Mile Road in the foothills just southeast of Santa Fe, has high ceilings and a wall of south-facing windows with expansive views. Overarched by an enormous sky, the long view is punctuated by the low triangular peaks of the Cerrillos Hills, the rugged Ortiz Mountains, the massive Sandia Mountains 60 miles away and the Galisteo Basin to the south. Closer in, waves of land dip into arroyos, and sand and rust-colored earth is dabbed with the dark green of piñon and juniper trees. Joel has placed his easel in clear view of the windows but out of reach of direct sunlight. He smilingly describes the space as his "indoor plein-air studio." It is here that his distinctive approach to landscape painting found its ongoing inspiration—in the land itself.

For a number of years Joel eschewed the use of photography as visual reference for his art. He believed it would somehow rob him of the creative possibilities available through direct observation, memory and imagination. As a result, the vocabulary of forms he began to develop were indeed inspired by specific experiences of storms, topographic landmarks and trees. But like his Modernist predecessors, Joel directs these elements in a dance of composition and color, moving beyond the constraints of realism to a joyful interplay of pattern and form. Layers of resonance emerge in paintings such as *Piñons and Hill* (1994) and *Desert Plants* (1992), where cloud shapes echo rock shapes and the geometry of hills repeats itself in what the artist fondly calls "generic triangle trees."

Endlessly moved by the vastness and timeless geologic feel of the earth and sky in this part of northern New Mexico, Joel in his early landscapes aims for what he considers the truth of the place. Clean shapes and strong angles speak of elemental nature in an ancient landscape. At the same time, the imagery contains a quiet quality and delicate color, offering the viewer an accessible sense of intimate, often lighthearted connection to the land. It is a reflection of the artist's own relationship to a place he has absorbed over a lifetime.

Glancing out the studio windows at a spreading, deeply hued sunset of gold and rose, Joel pauses in his conversation. "When you look out the windows every evening at something like this," he reflects, "it's an integral part of your life."

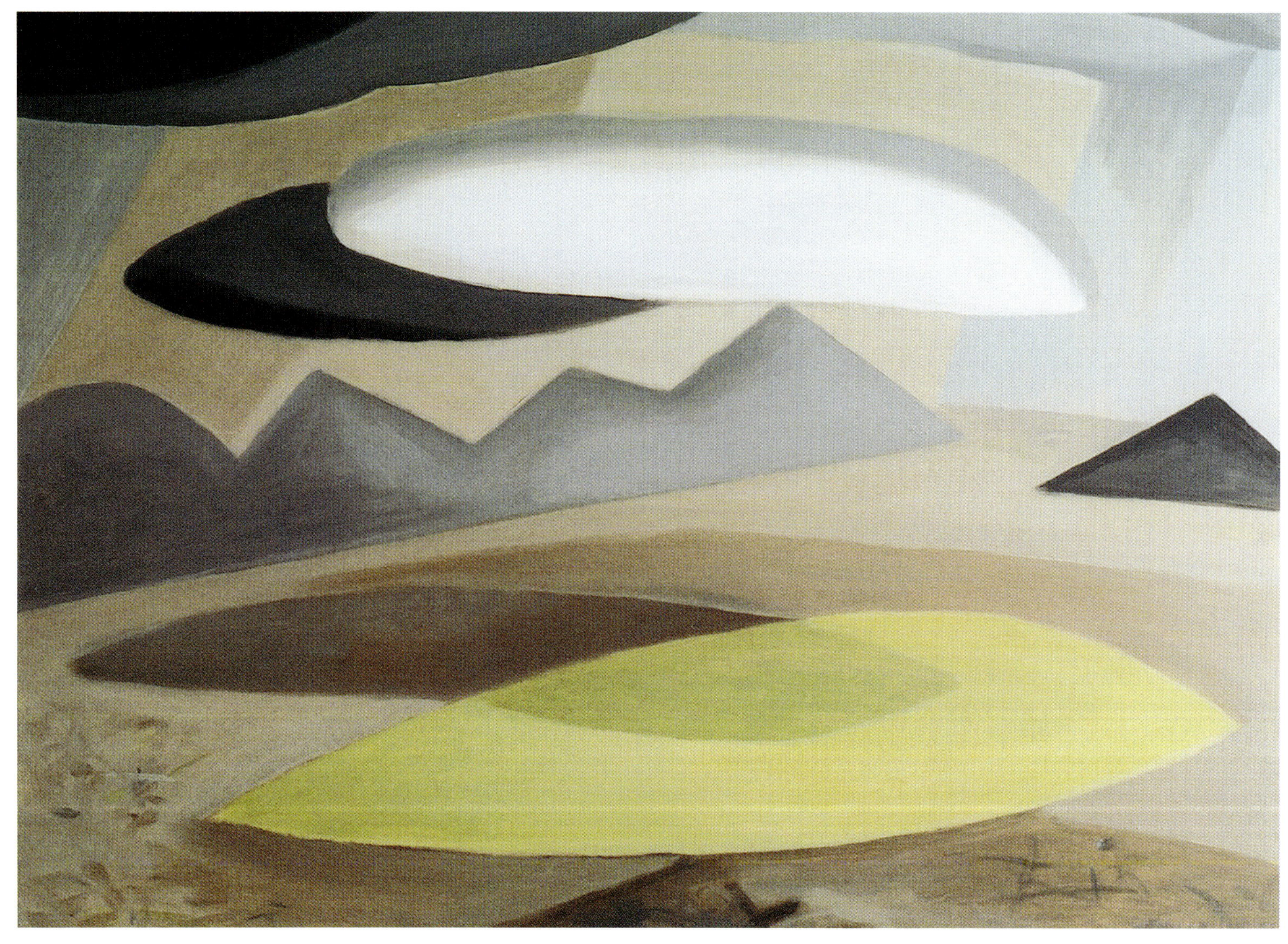

Cloud Shadows, 1991 Oil on board, 17" × 24"

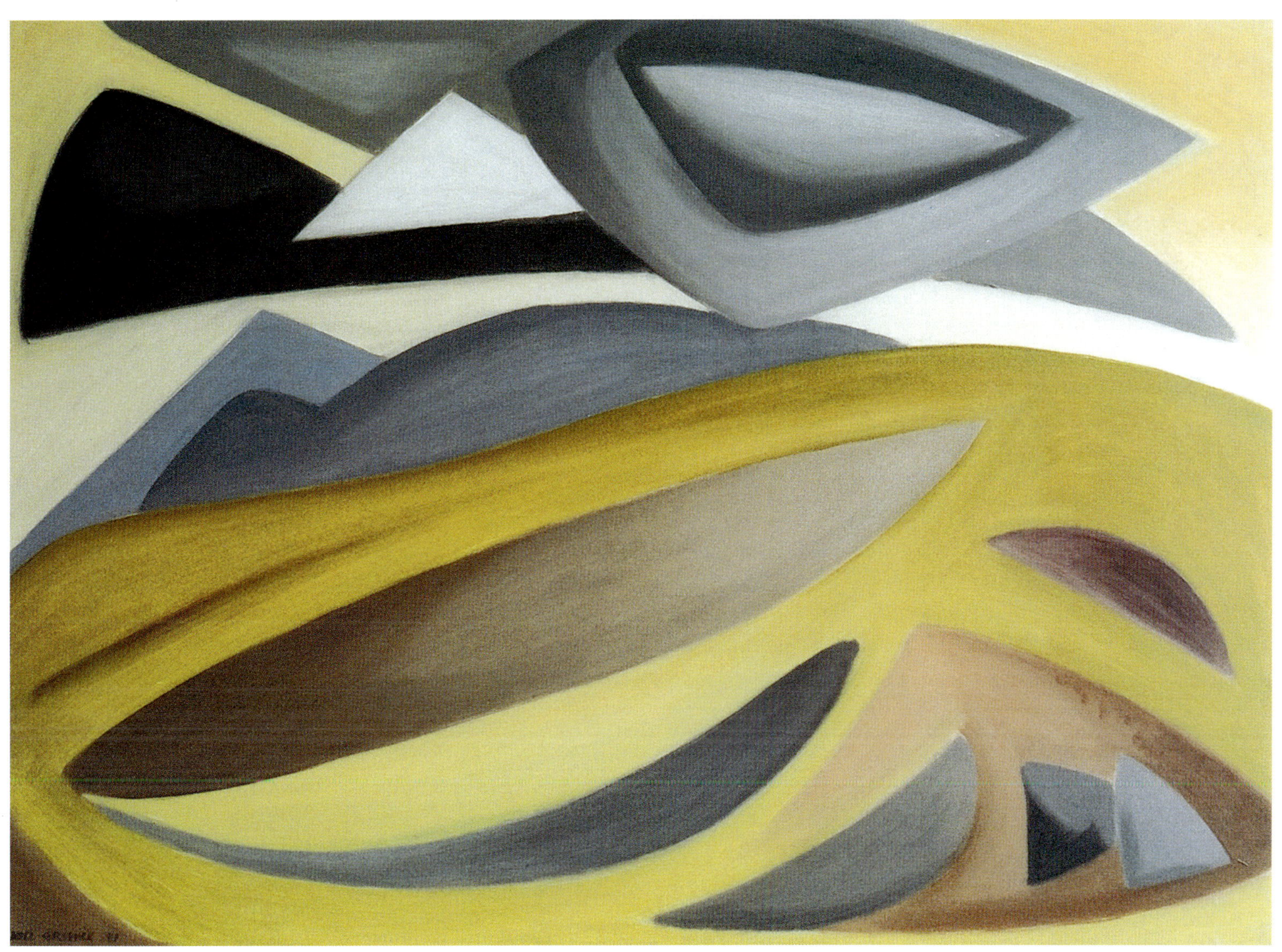

Gash, 1991

Oil on board, 17" × 24"

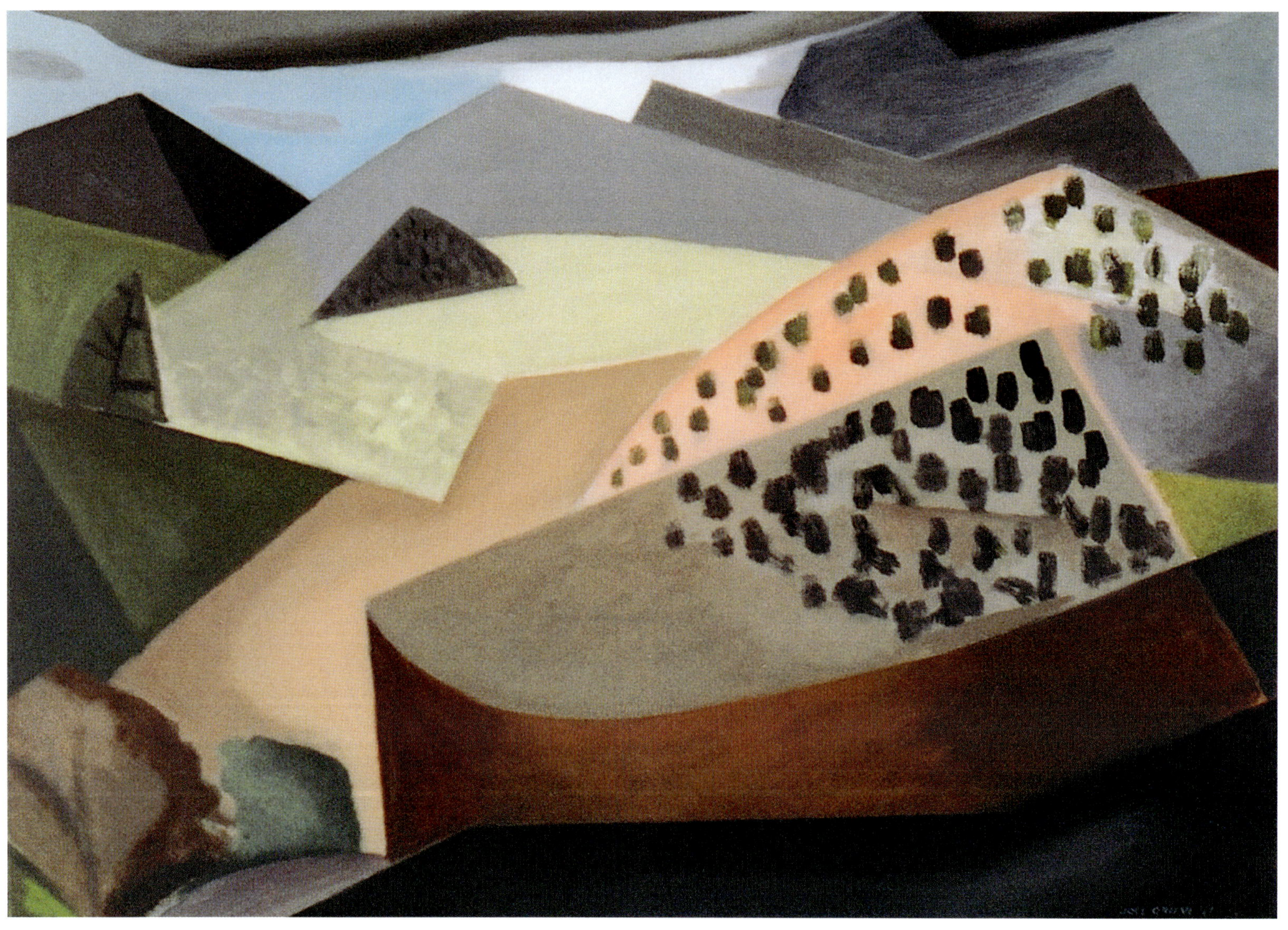

Landscape, 1991

Oil on board, 17" × 24"

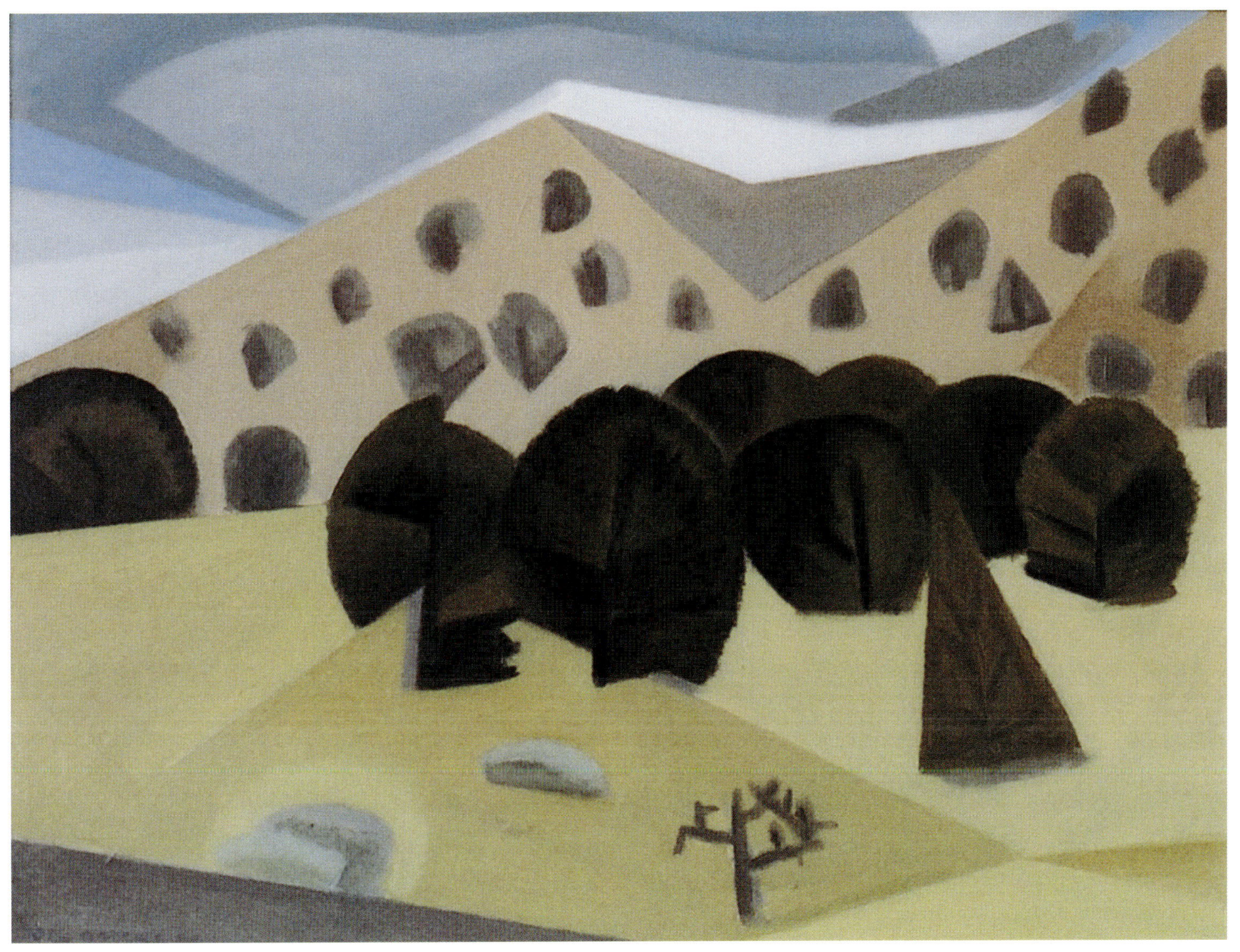

Piñons and Hill, 1994

Oil on board, 12" × 16"

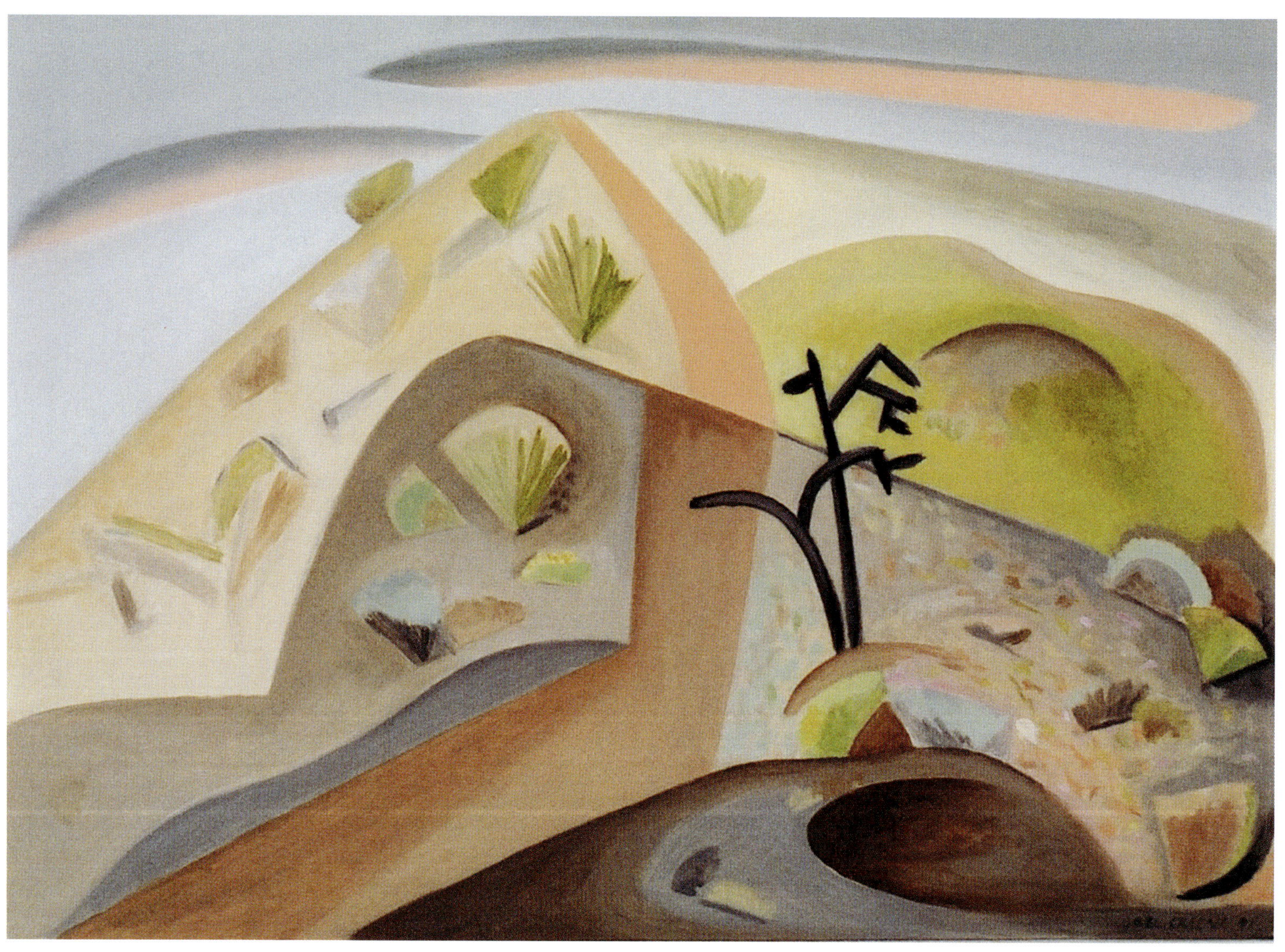

Desert Plants, 1991

Oil on board, 17" × 24"

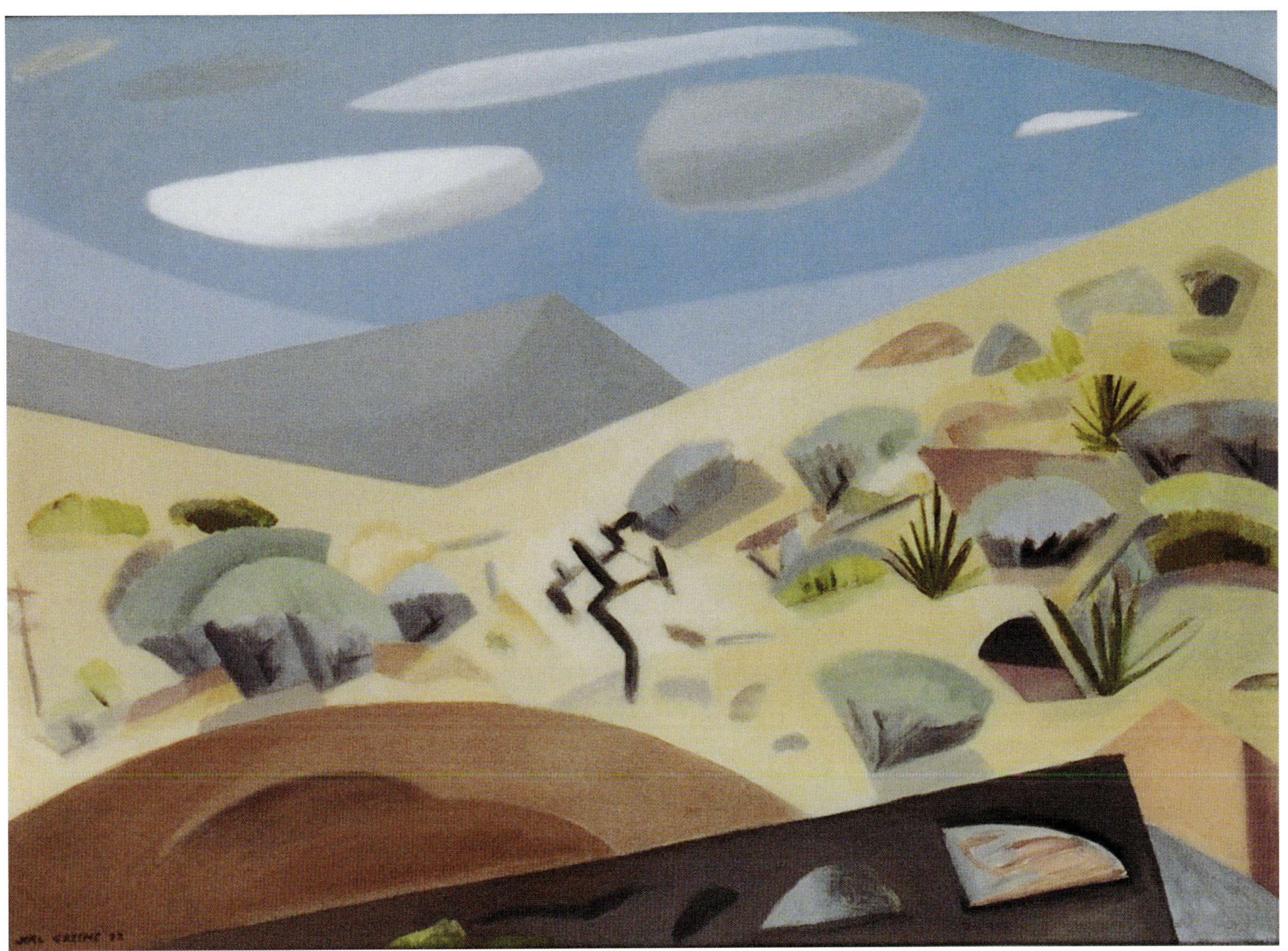

Desert Plants, 1992

Oil on board, 17" × 24"

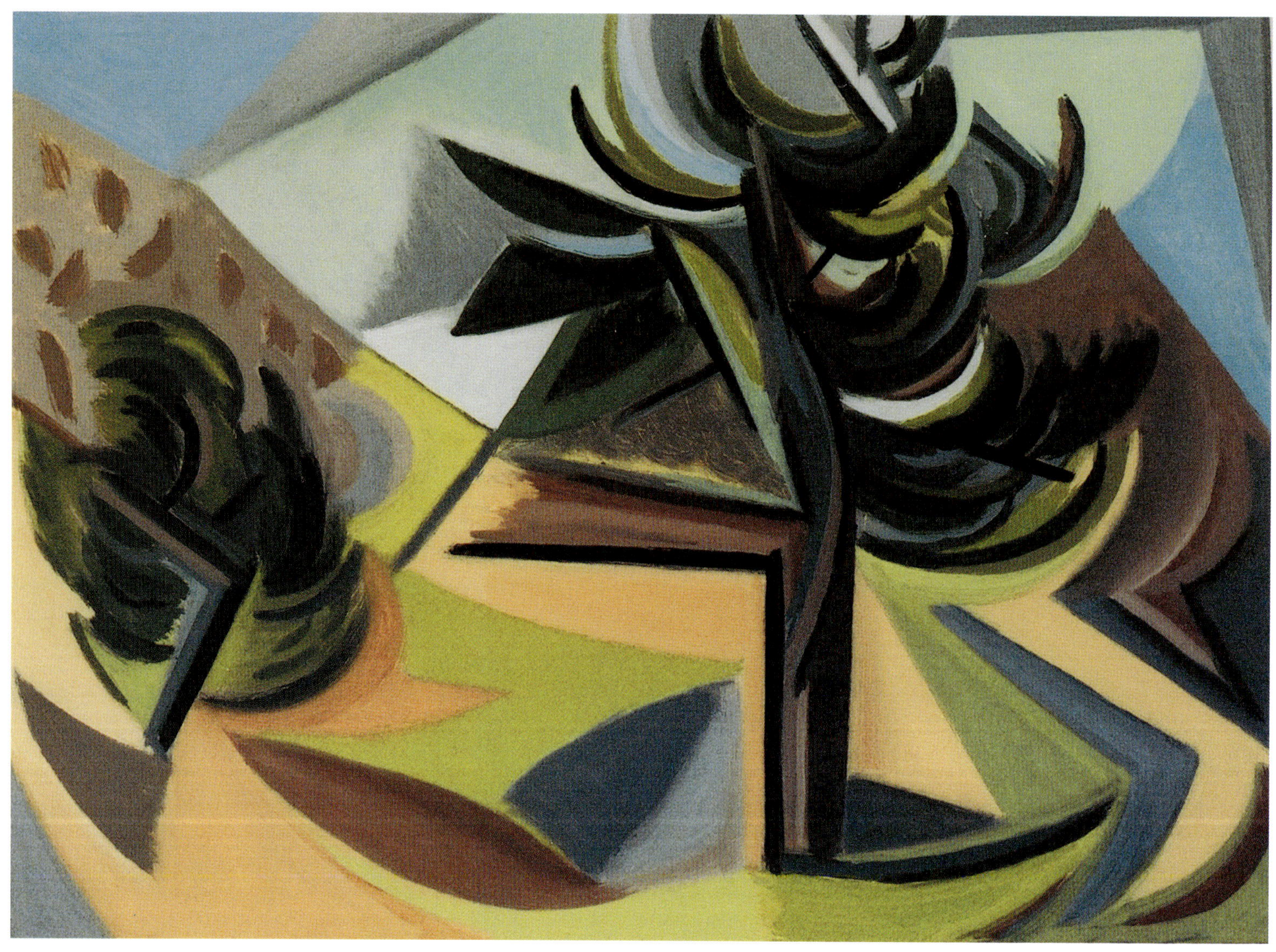

Piñons, 1998

Oil on board, 8" × 11"

evolution of the tree

Gosh, what a world we'd have if we didn't have trees. —Joel Greene

Those who have never seen New Mexico may imagine it as a barren, sun-beaten desert land. Those familiar with the state, and with northern New Mexico in particular, know the region to be blessed with trees: the hardy juniper and slow-growing, shapely piñon; shady, river-loving cottonwoods; and high-altitude aspen, ponderosa pine and spruce. New Mexicans cherish the presence of trees and mourn the ones that don't survive, especially in years of drought.

But for Joel, the tree offers another dimension as well. In it he finds a living confluence between the world outdoors and his long-held admiration for the Cubist approach to color and form. Opening an art-history book, he turns to *Picasso's Landscape* (1908) and the early works of Braque, such as *Road Near L'Estaque* (1908). "It's these curves, the straight lines, the little triangles—I'm playing with these," he explains, pointing to the Cubist depiction of trees. "These are my colors too! I love those colors. It think this was just an incredible period of art. It's really the foundation of what I'm doing, even though my work now is less rigidly geometric and more sinuous. Eventually you realize you can't do exactly what these artists did, but you make something of your own. And that takes developing a level of confidence and a language."

The tree has been a vital and evolving form in Joel's artistic vocabulary. From the angular, interlocking complexity of a Cubist perspective (seen in *Piñon III* and *Piñon IV*), his focus gradually turned toward the clean simplicity expressed in works such as *Piñons and Junipers* (1996) and *Piñons and Heavy Sky* (2001). Along the way his conversation with the canvas took on a new, more personalized tone. His profound inspiration from the work of earlier artists served as a seed in the unfolding of his signature abstractionist style as he matured as an artist. Yet through every phase of his work, both his background in art history and his direct observation of the world have been translated into imagery by means of an intuitive approach. Whether precisely guiding a burin, an engraving tool, across a copper plate or wielding brushes and paint, Joel starts with a foundation of accumulated knowledge and experience. Then he moves into a process of wordless, purposeful engagement in the depiction of even the most ordinary of subjects, like the tree.

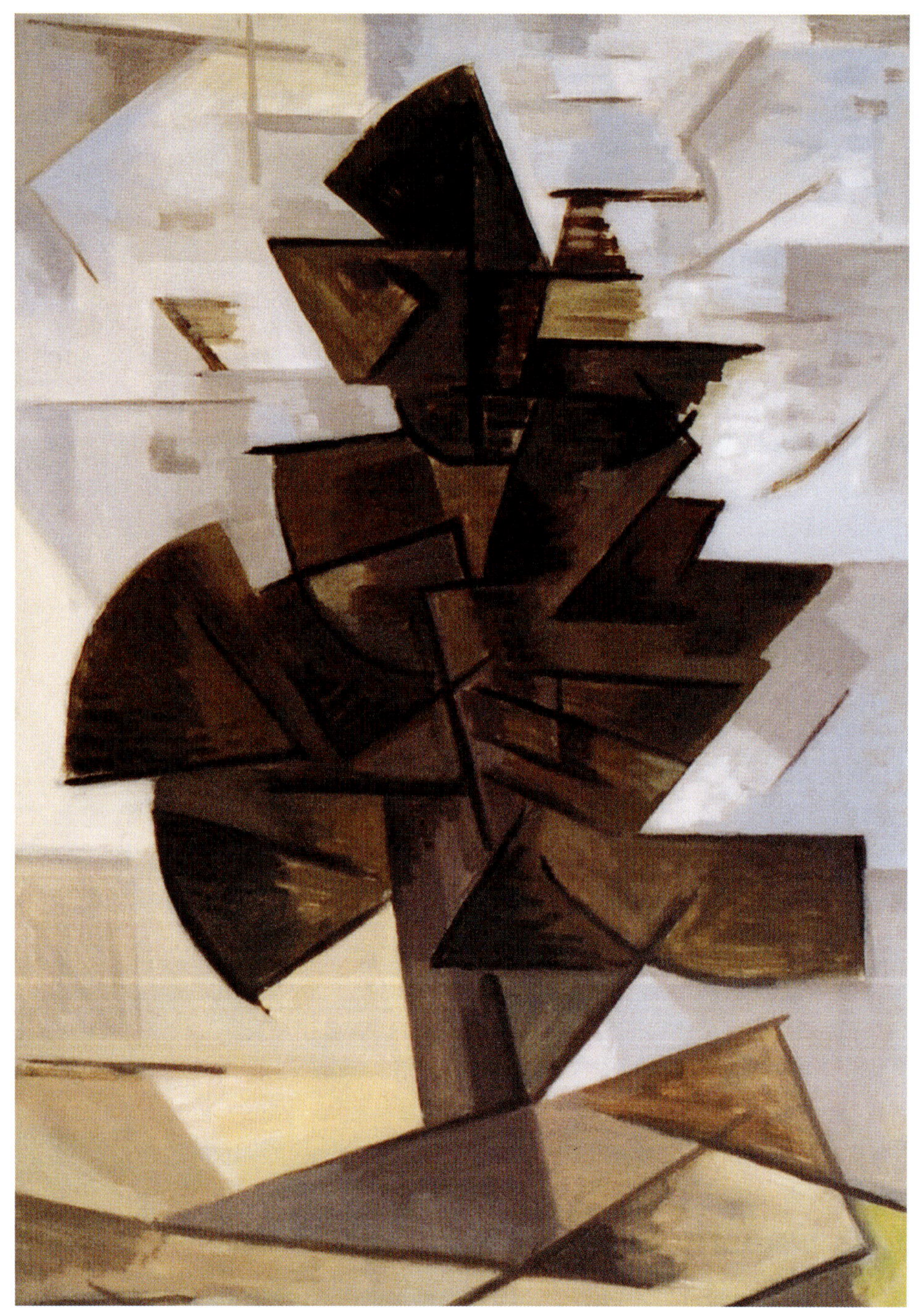

Piñon III, 1994
Oil on board, 24" × 17"

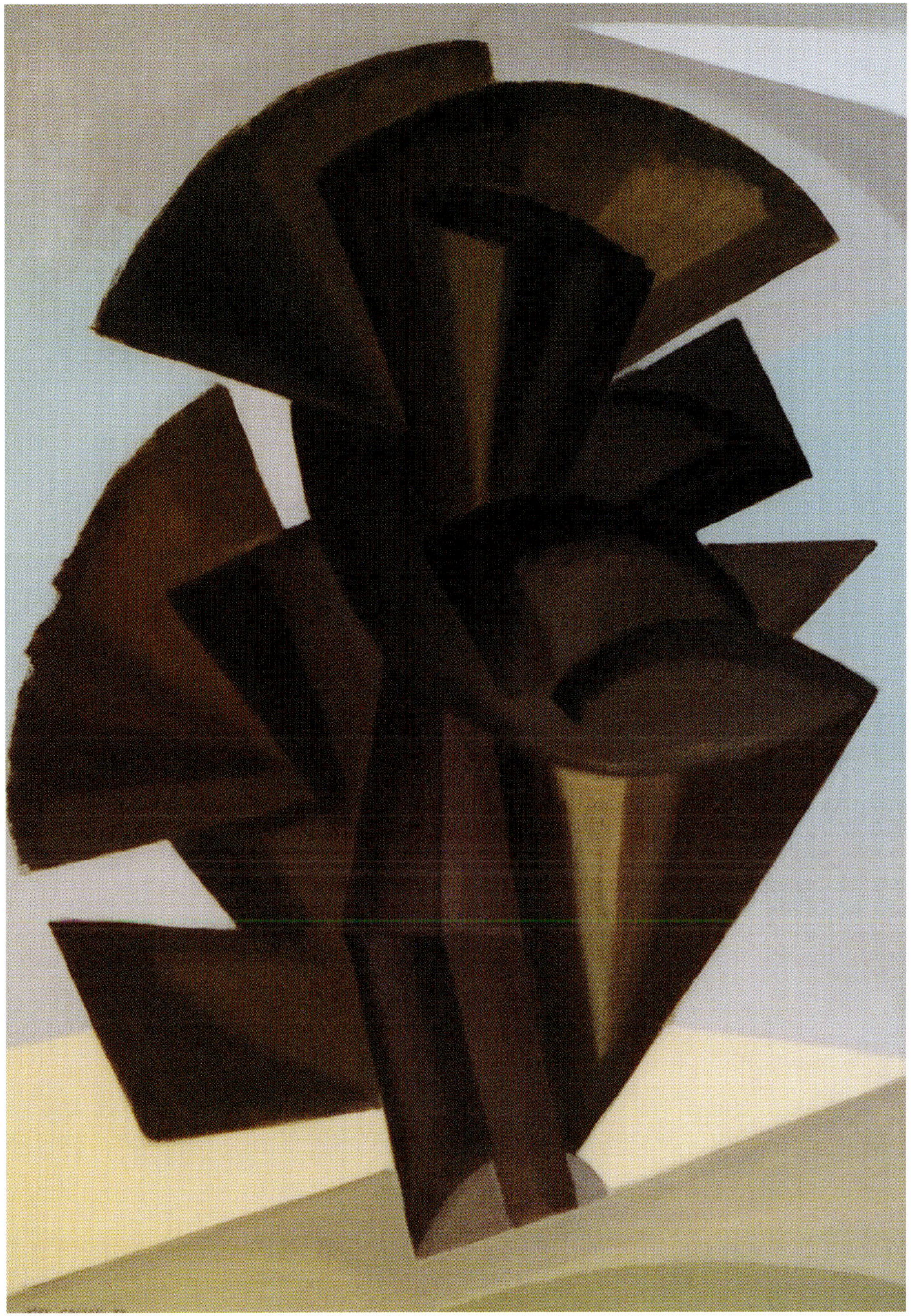

Piñon IV, 1994
Oil on board, 24" × 17"

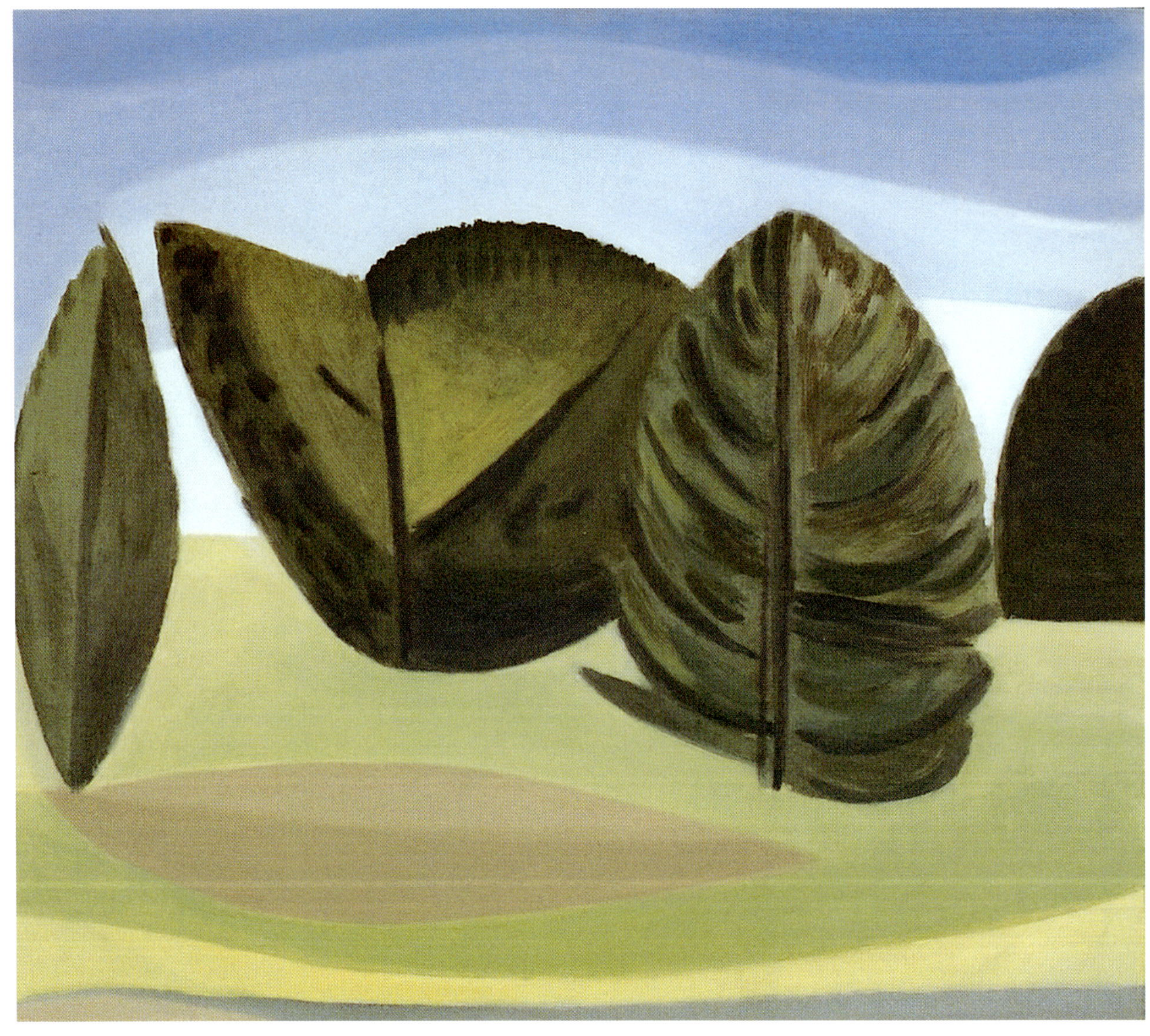

Piñons and Junipers, 1996 Oil on board, 10" × 11 ½"

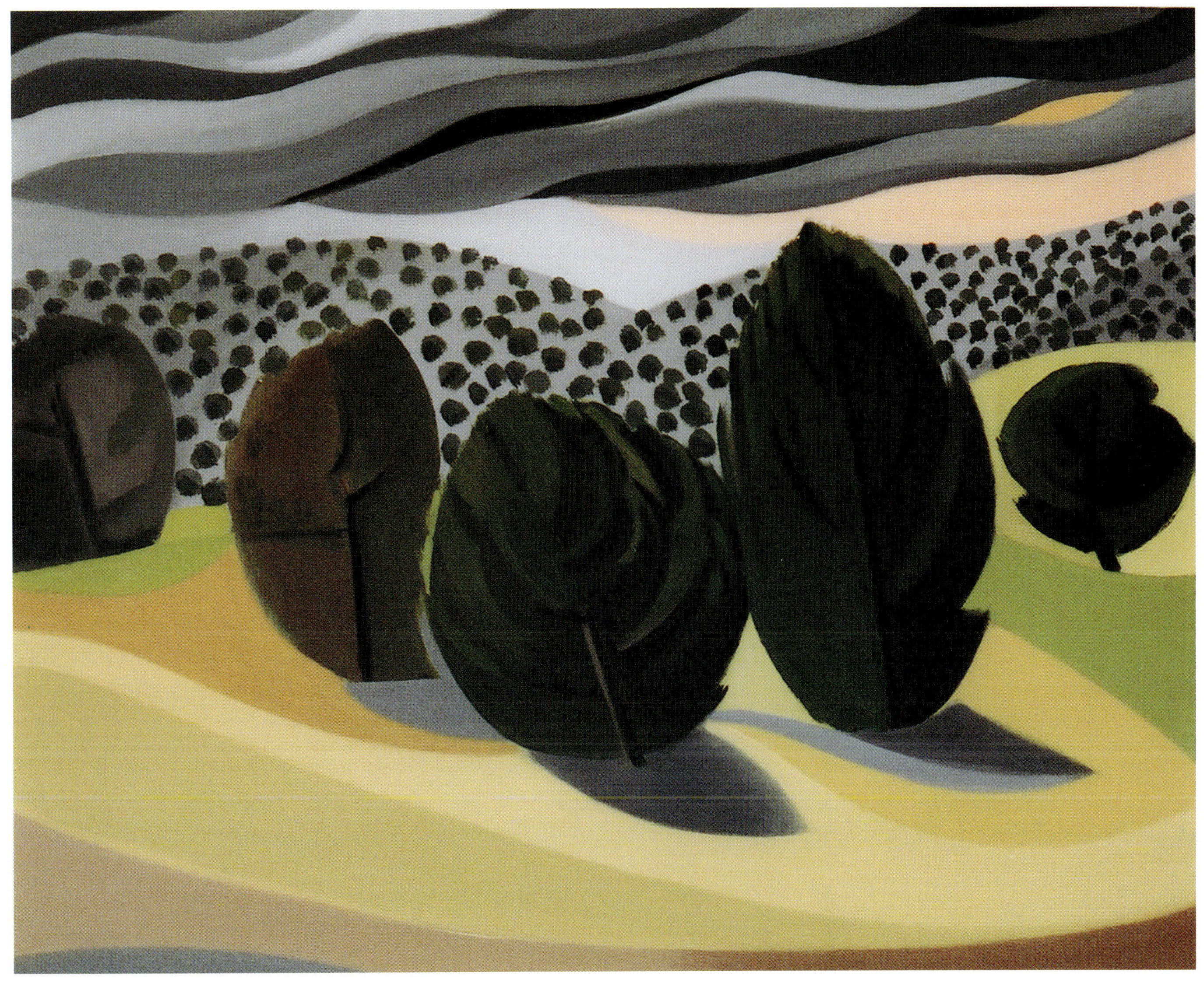

Piñons and Heavy Sky, 2001

Oil on board, 13" × 16 ¼"

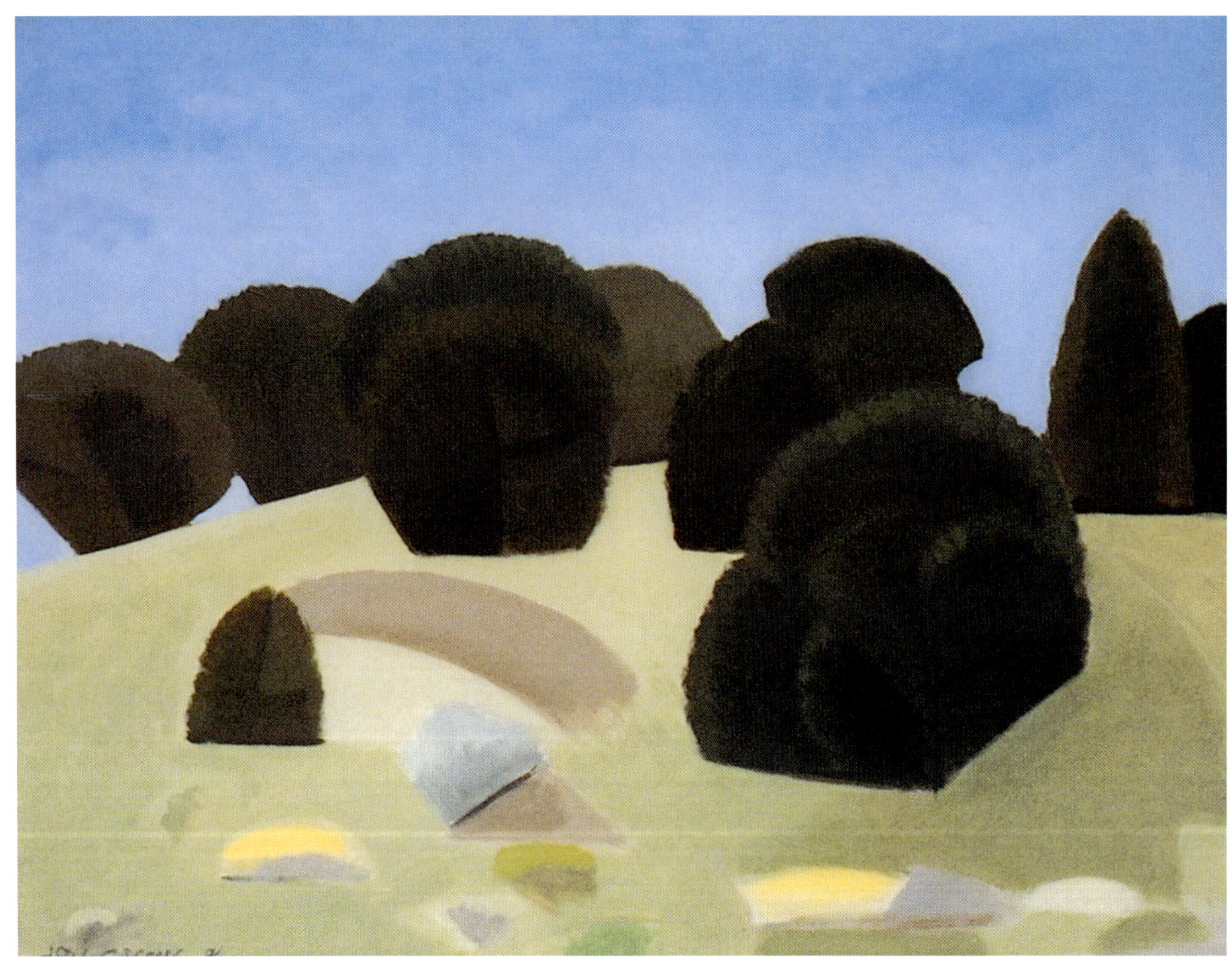

Piñons, 1996 Oil on board, 10" × 13"

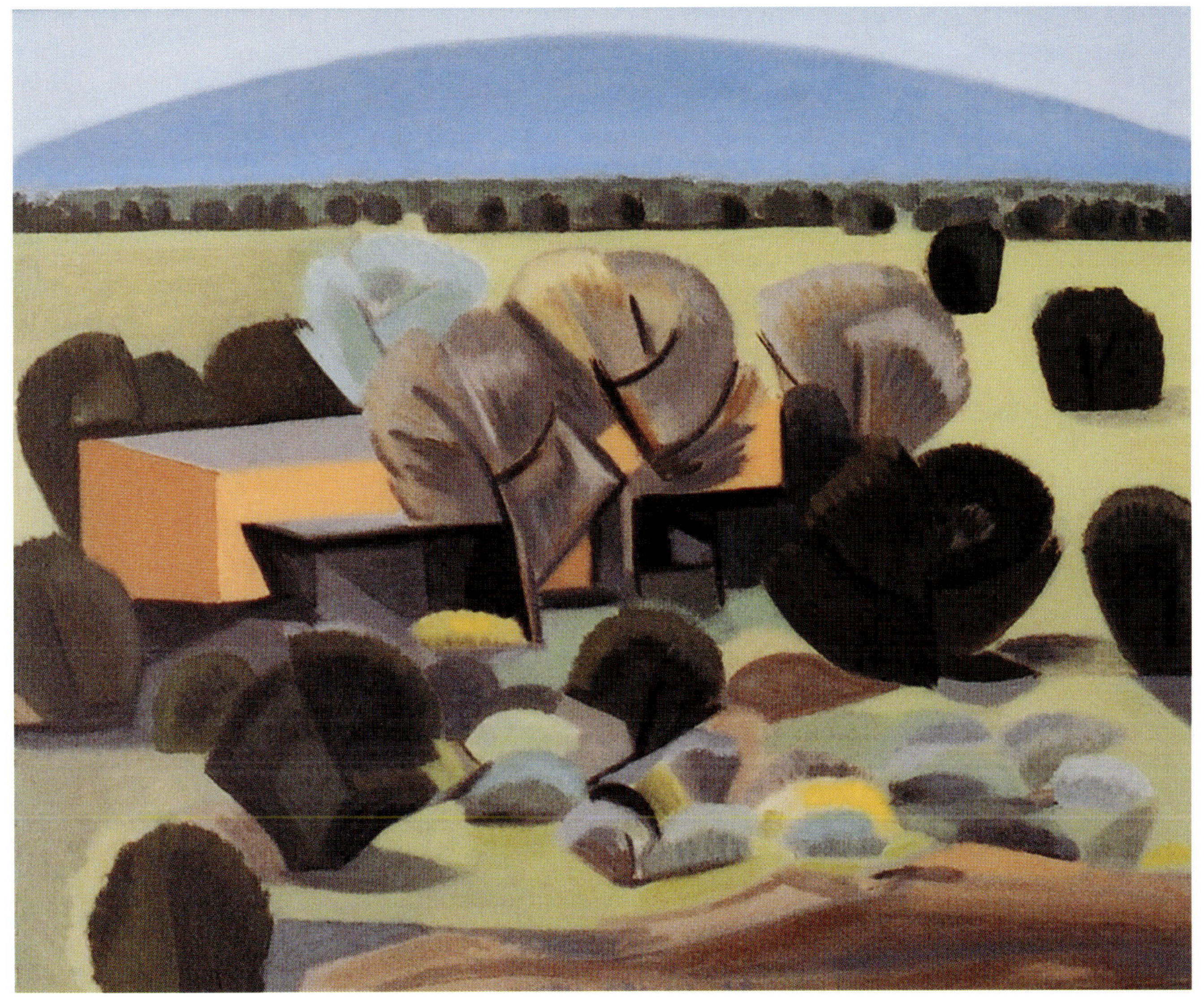

House and Piñons, 1998

Oil on board, 10" × 12 ¼"

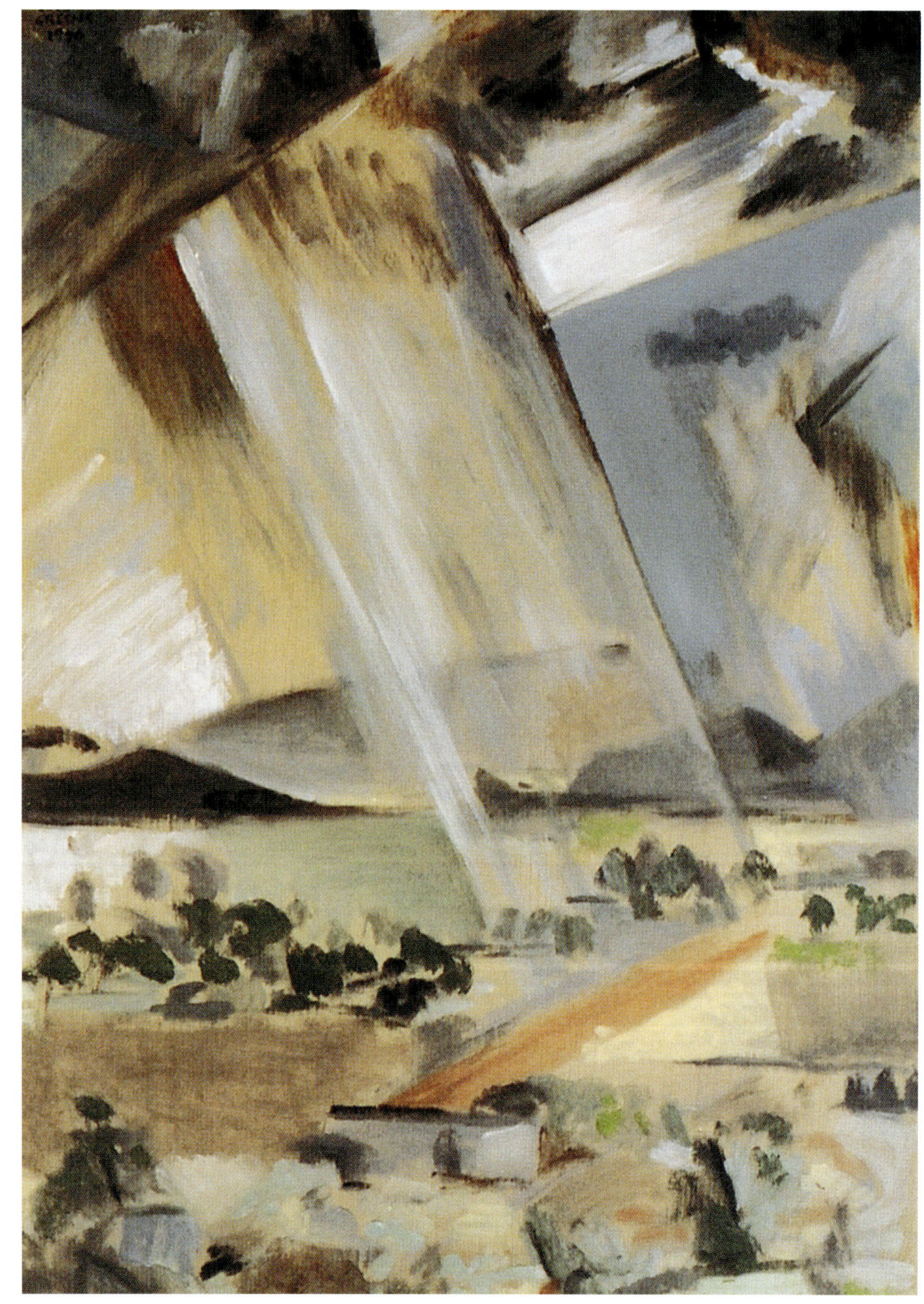

Rain, 1991
Oil on board, 18" × 13"

stormy weather

I was taking a walk and the sky was really like that! It was the most extraordinary thing. —Joel Greene

Joel has a white Miata convertible sports car. On summer days he climbs in and heads off, nothing between himself and the magnificent, ever-changing meteorological show overhead. The energy and vertical vastness of billowing thunderheads, the spectacle of watching several storms across the horizon at once, the rush of storm-born wind—New Mexico's legendary skies can instill a feeling of awe in anyone. But for an artist whose instruments of composition are visual jazz and eloquent shape, the skyward view is truly heaven hovering close to earth.

Translating such an experience onto a two-dimensional surface, however, is a challenge shared by artists throughout time. Some of Joel's early paintings and prints of spectacular weather suggest a particular affinity with the New Mexico Modernists of the early 1900s. In *Rain* (1991), for instance, we sense an echo of John Marin's watercolor scenes and Andrew Dasburg's impressionistic approach, where quick suggestions of vegetation, hills and rain project a feeling of drama and space.

Later Joel moved through a phase of more broadly angular and geometric depictions of stormy skies. In these works, especially, we understand the term *walking rain*, often used by longtime New Mexicans to describe tall gray columns of rain that make their way across the landscape.

In the decade between 1990 and 2000, a gracefully fluid, swirling feel found its way into Joel's imagery, replacing, for the most part, the straight lines and corners of his earlier work. The shift represented the artist's growing interest in a more naturalistic approach to the landscape, while still maintaining and developing a personal stylized vocabulary of color and forms. *Sunlit Hills* and *Rain, Highway 41*, both from 2002, also reflect an increasing refinement of color gradations that characterize his more recent work.

As Joel describes it, the act of painting stormscapes (or any subject) is a flowing, organic process itself. "I start with something that strikes me—the way shapes look against each other, the rhythm of things, how they echo," he explains. "I mix up a little gray and do a rough outline and then just start painting. The tones and colors don't really show up until I start building up layers and figuring out what's going on with it. At a certain point I forget the photos and sketches and what I'm actually seeing and let the shapes in the painting, the spaces, tones and colors develop on their own."

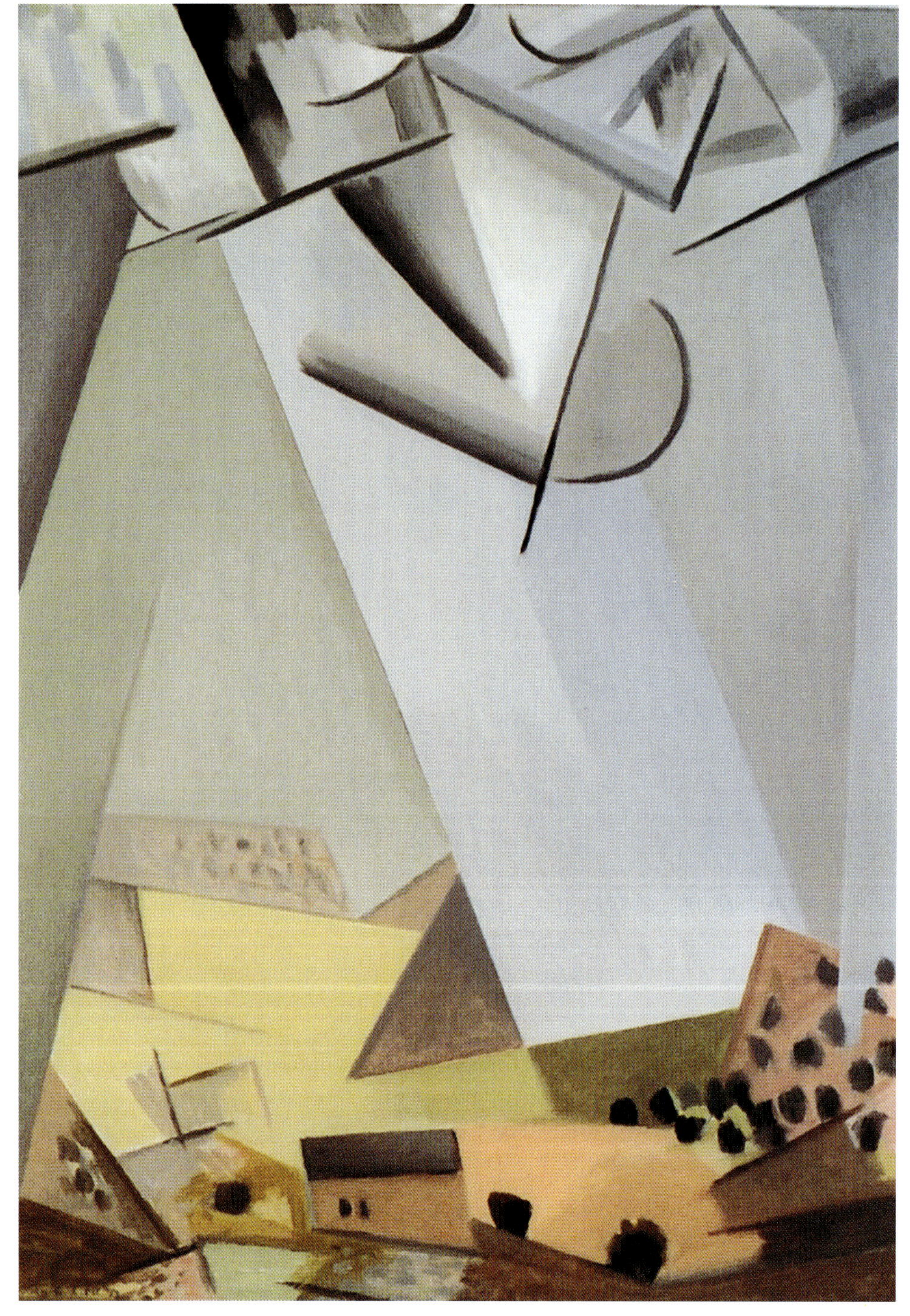

Rain, 1991
Oil on board, 24" × 17"

Lightning, 1992
Oil on linen, 30" × 22"

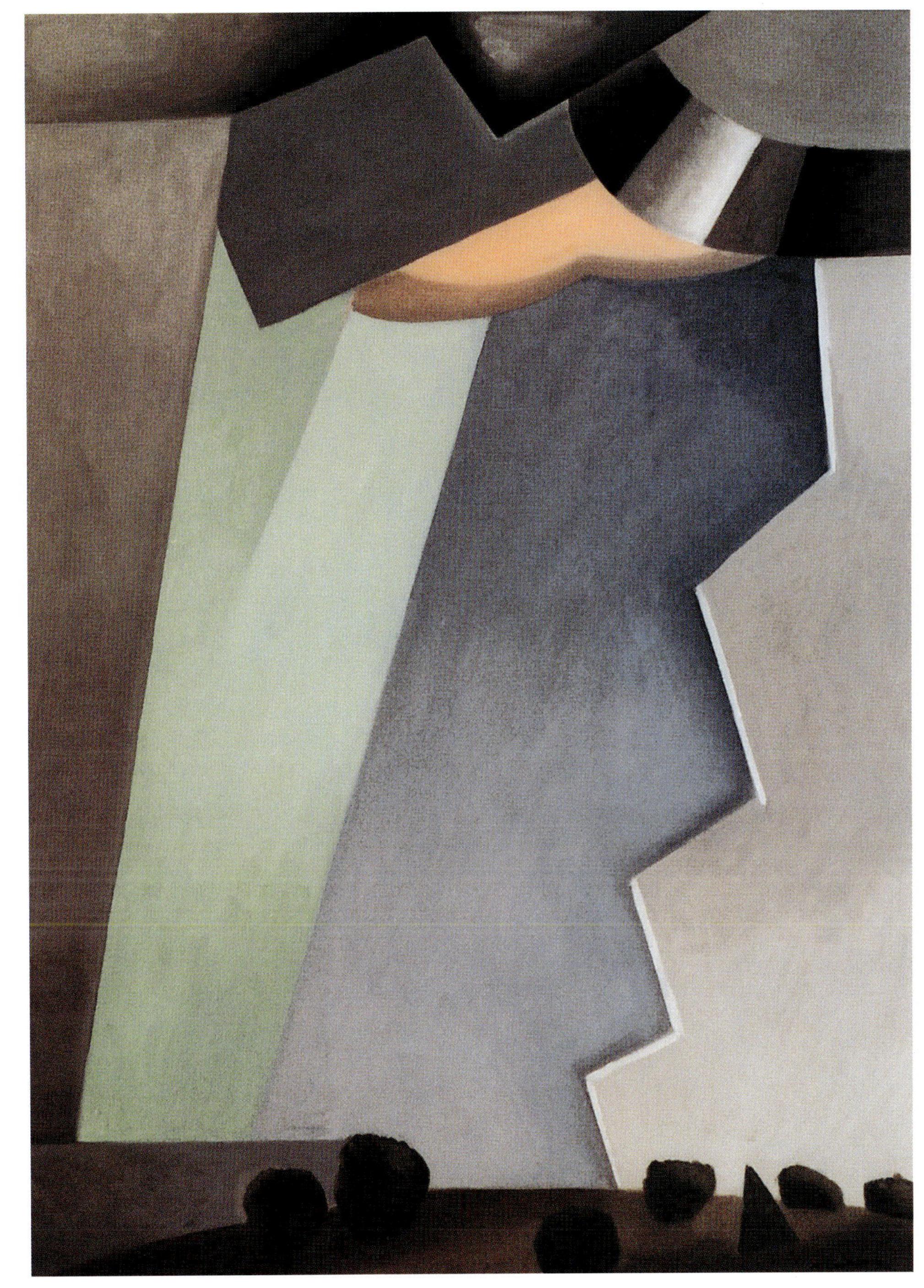

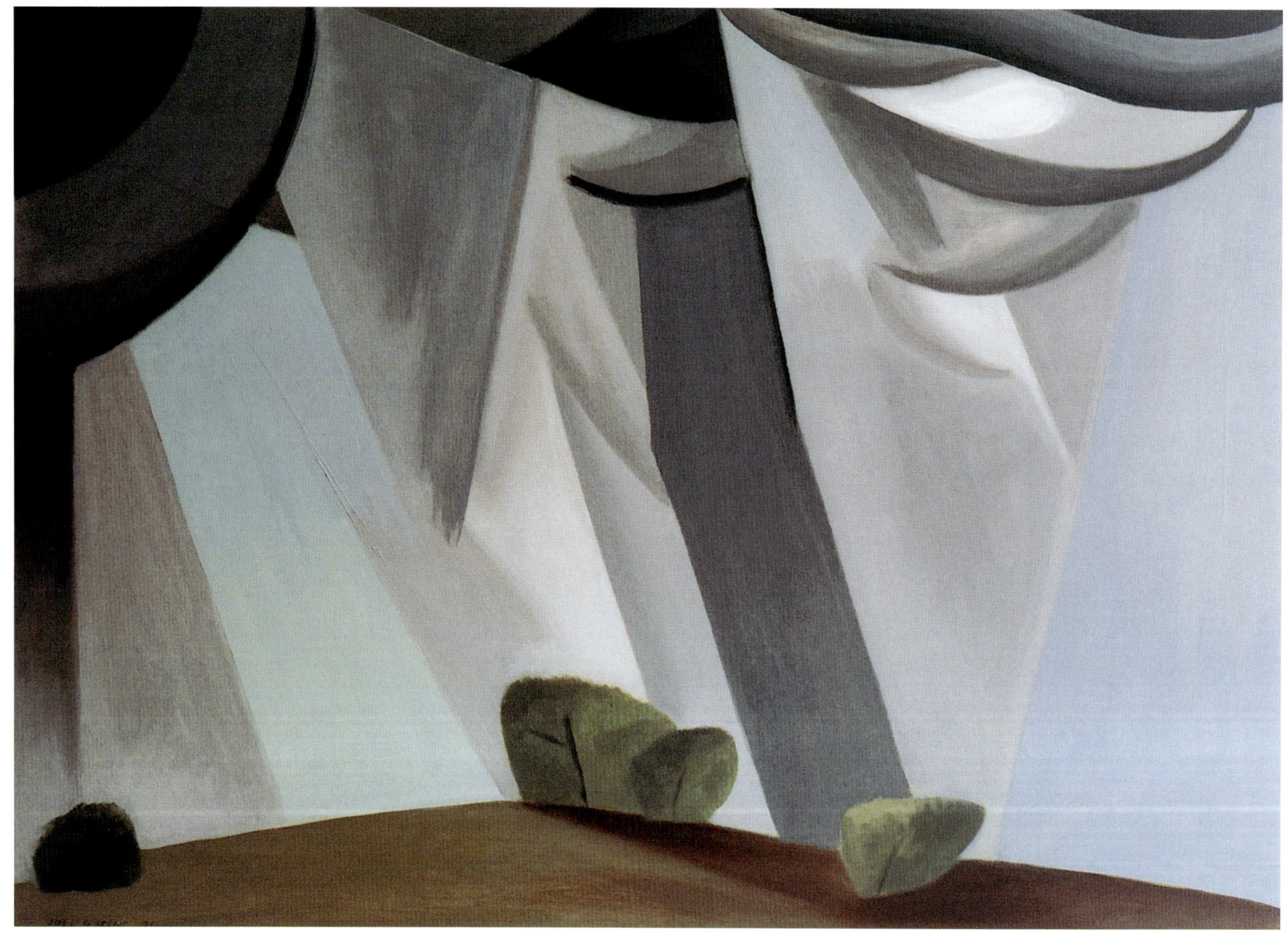

Rain, 1991 Oil on board, 17" × 24"

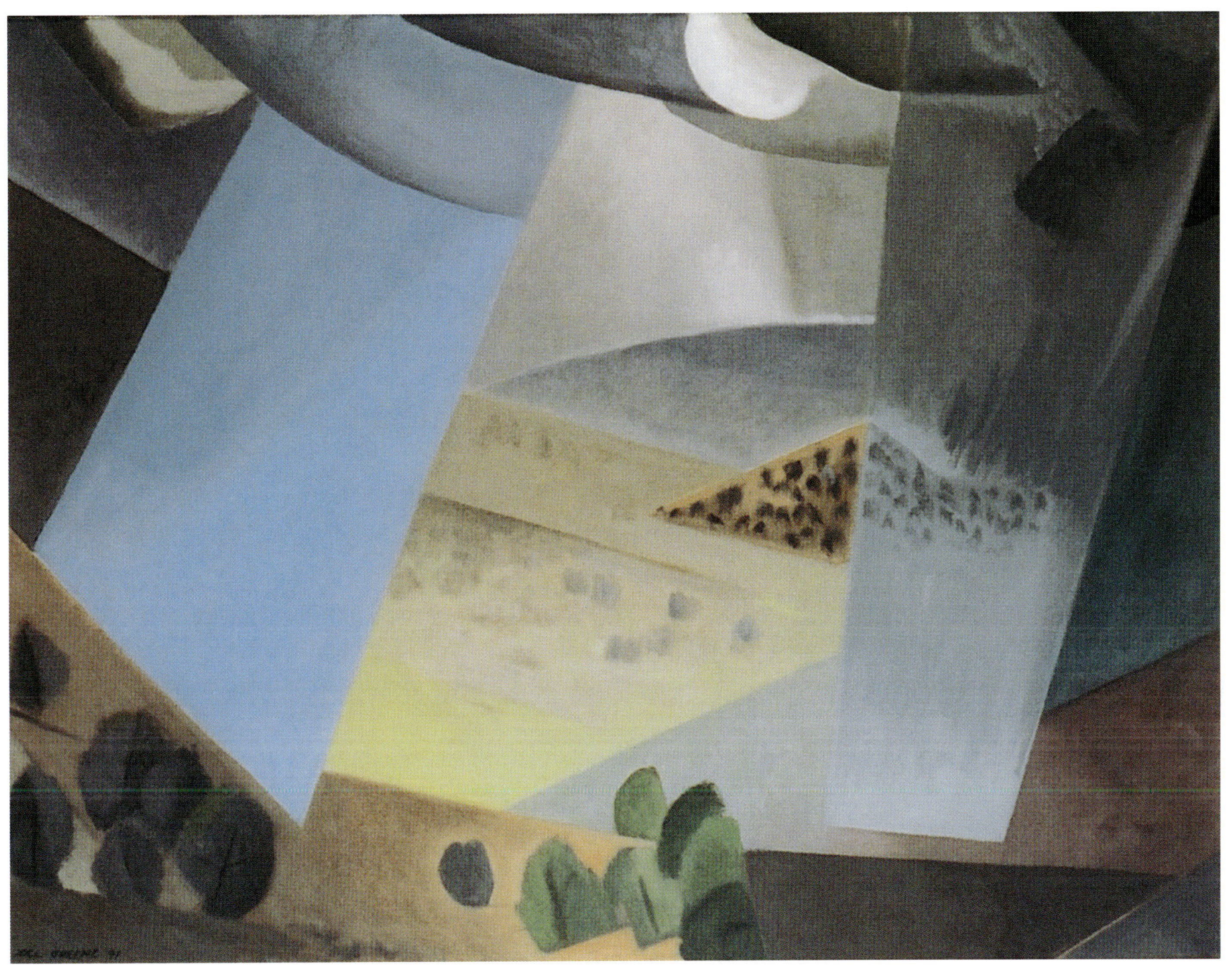

Rainstorm, 1991 — Oil on linen, 18" × 24"

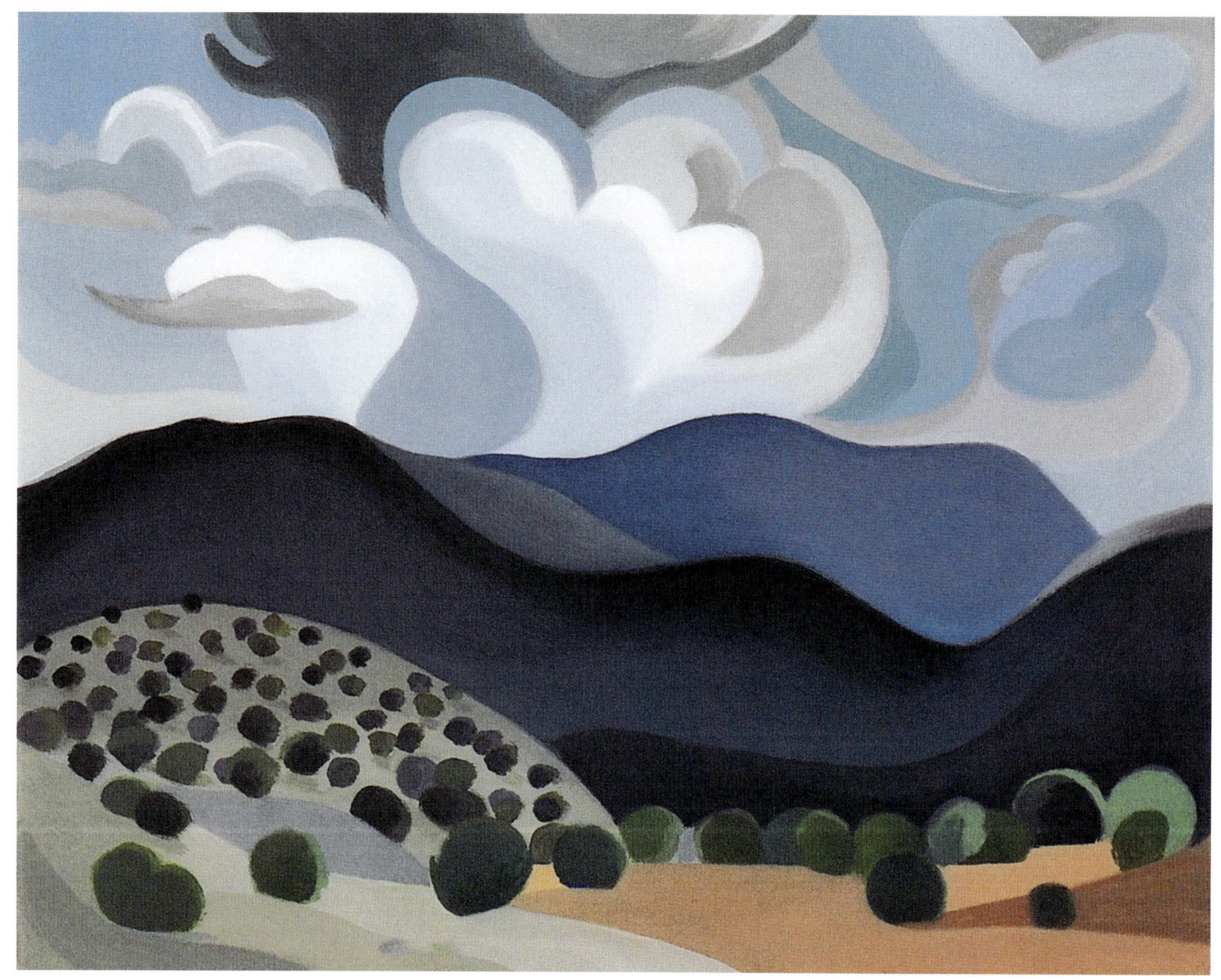

Sunlit Hills, 2002

Oil on board, 11" × 14"

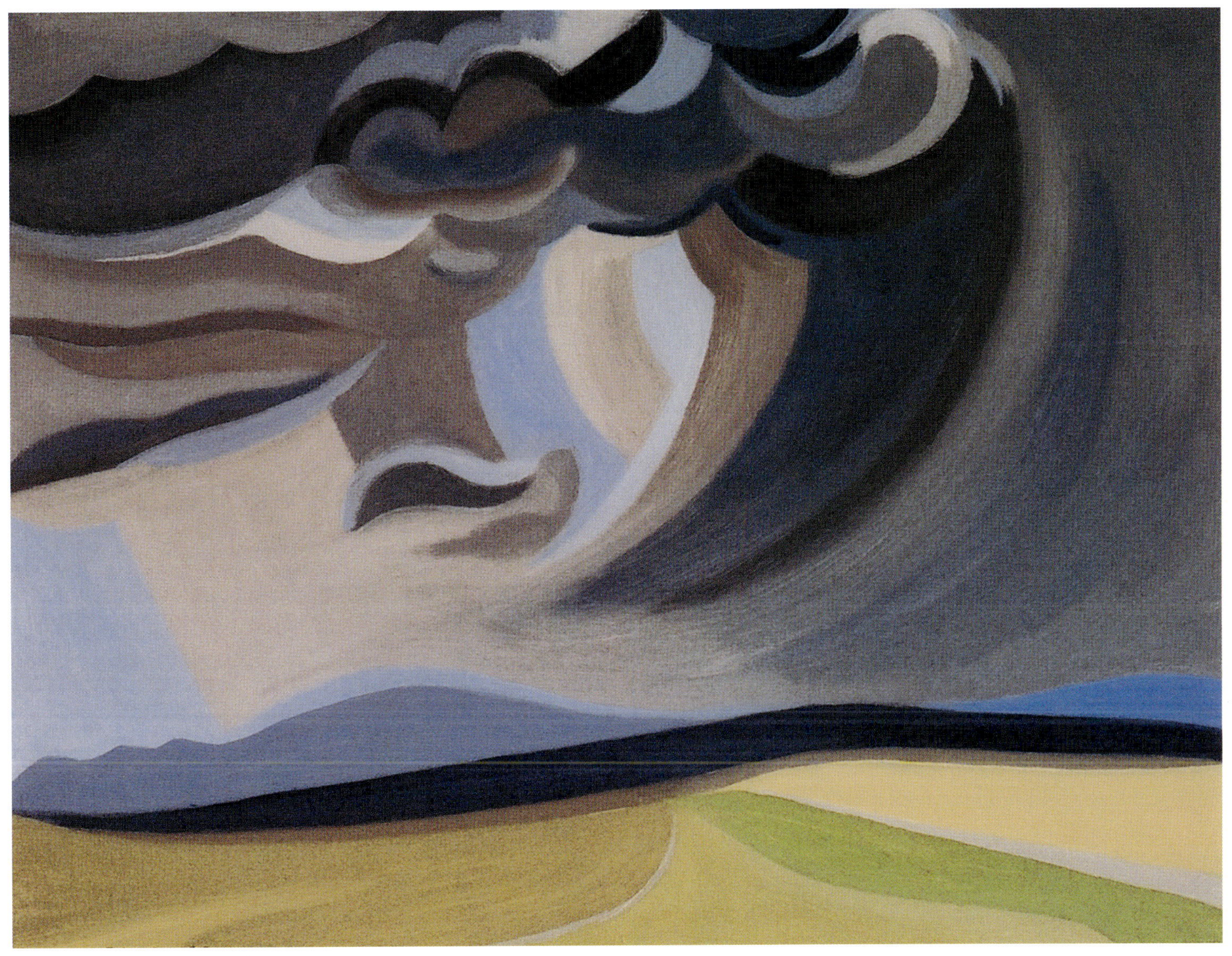

Rain, Highway 41, 2002 Oil on board, 9" × 12"

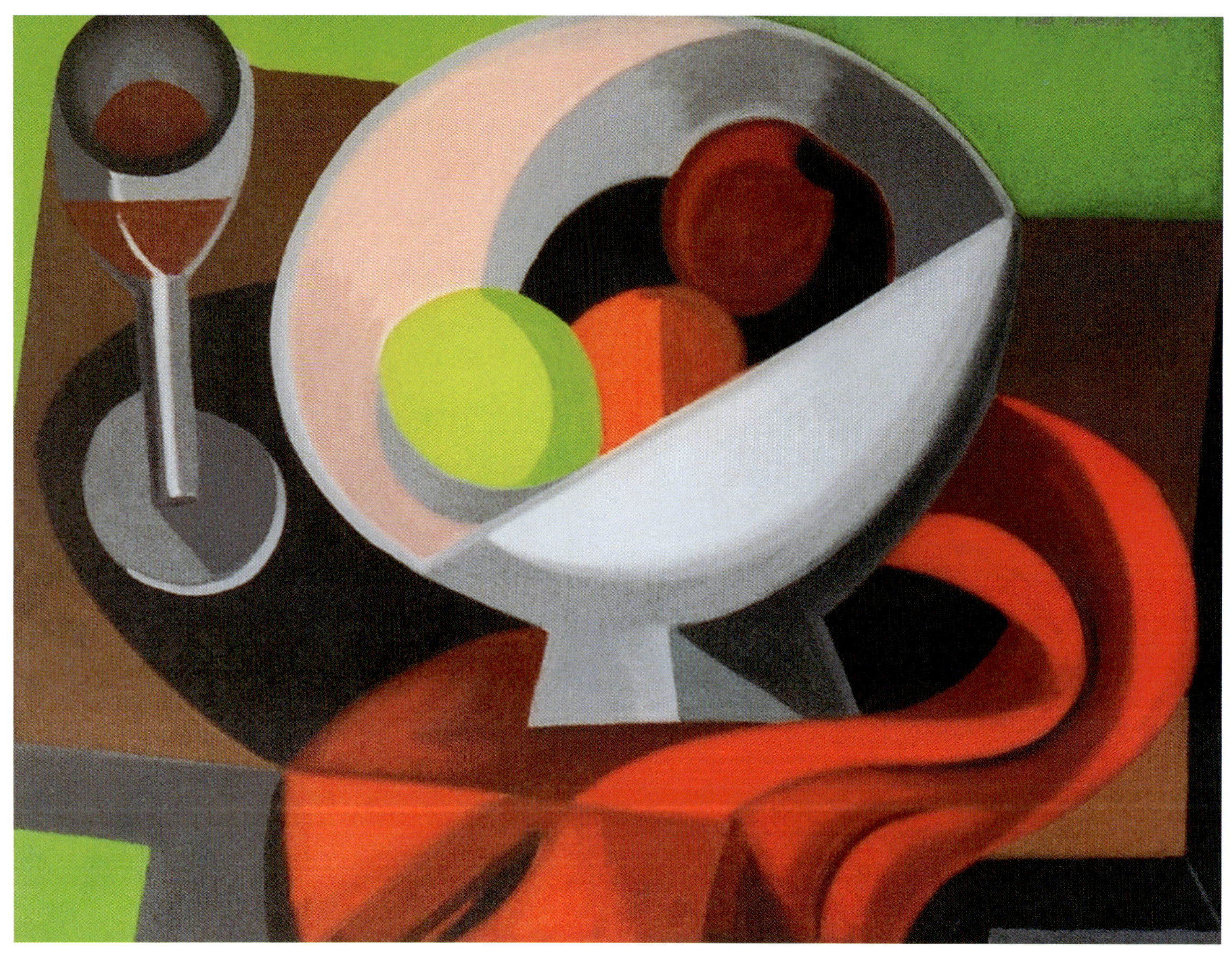

Fruit and Glass of Wine, 1996 — Oil on board, 12" × 16"

still life with fun

Objects have such a presence, the way they sit in the space. —Joel Greene

If the picture plane is a playing field, Joel changes games from time to time. His still life phase is one of "rampant Cubism," as he puts it, where all the elements he enjoys from that period of art can be expressed in self-challenging exploration and delight. "Cubism lends itself to still life, and still life is an exercise, a way of getting at the problems of making a painting," he explains. "I like the fracture, the busy surface. It's a way of making your eye go across the painting and deep into it and up to the surface again, it's lines playing against each other. You can see that thrust of a line, where it gets carried through, then gets broken off, then starts again. To me, those things are more important than having a painting tell a story."

In its long history as an artistic genre, the still life frequently has been instilled with the import of collective and personal meaning, from social and religious symbolism to the universal reminder of human mortality in 17th-century Dutch *vanitas* pieces. While respecting this long tradition and its value in other artists' work, Joel sees his own still-life painting as deliberately sidestepping symbolism in favor of the purity of shape and color that objects can provide. Still, the objects he chooses come from his everyday life. As such, a form of personal symbolism—what one collector calls the "poetry of the daily"—is inherent in this imagery, containing as it does a bit of Joel: his tea tin, a beer glass, his pipe from days gone by.

More importantly, the still-life genre offers another arena for the forms, and their interaction with each other, that find expression in all of Joel's work. Instead of "triangle trees" and hills, there are table edges and triangular pieces of fruit. Instead of clouds we find a flowing tablecloth and the curves of glasses and bowls. And, not surprisingly, we may find a touch of humor going on. "There's a five-sided table," the artist says of *Plant, Blue Cloth and Window*. "But it's so subtle—that's the fun thing; you don't notice it has five sides.

"There's a certain freedom Cubism gives you to organize things differently and make new shapes." This freedom extends to the still-life setup as well. Rather than gathering and carefully placing objects, he arranges and designs as he paints. The individual aloe plant or lemon is there for reference. But the game is putting them together in simple, yet fresh and inventive ways.

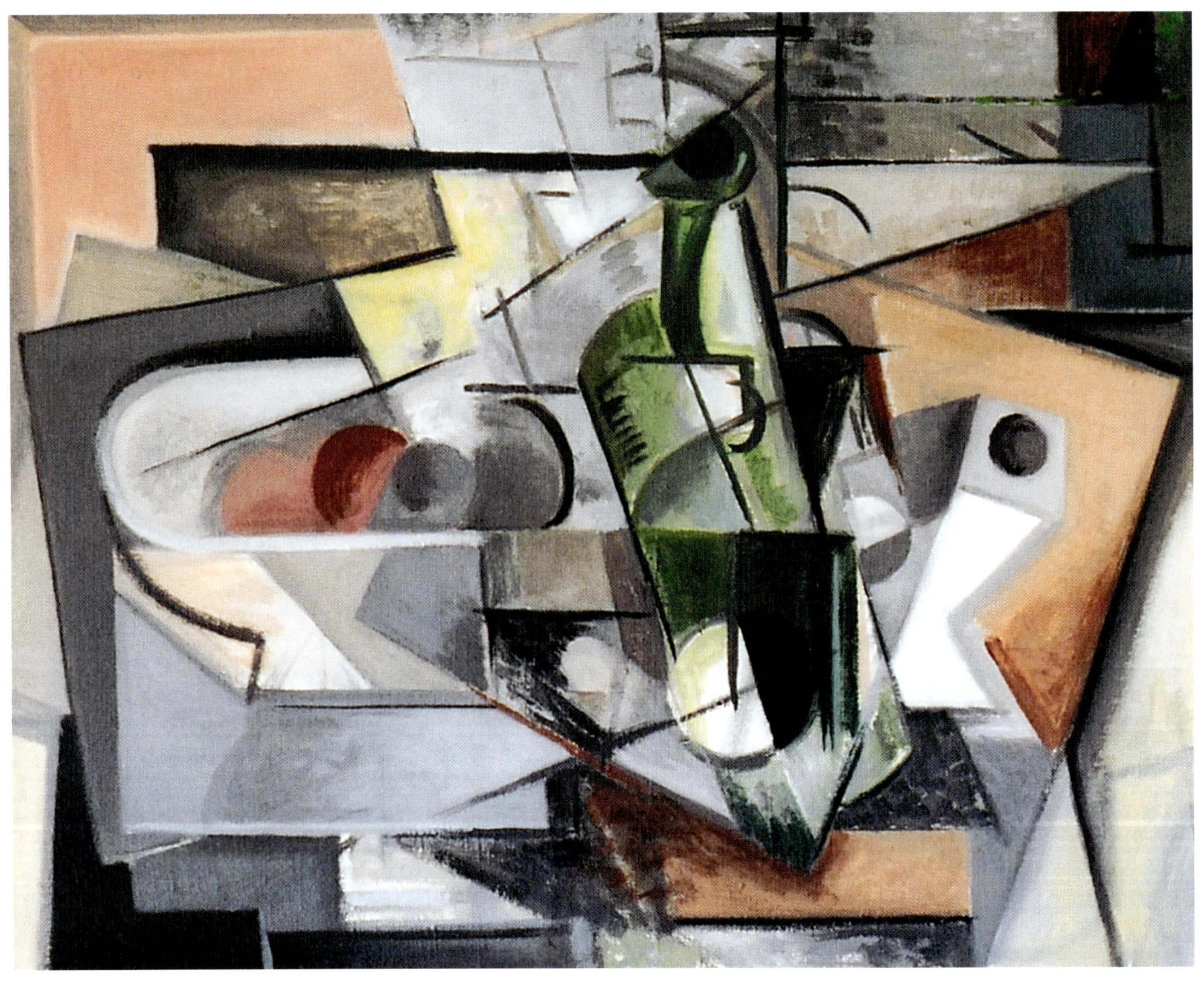

Fruit Bowl, Glass and Bottle, 1989 Oil on board, 16" × 20"

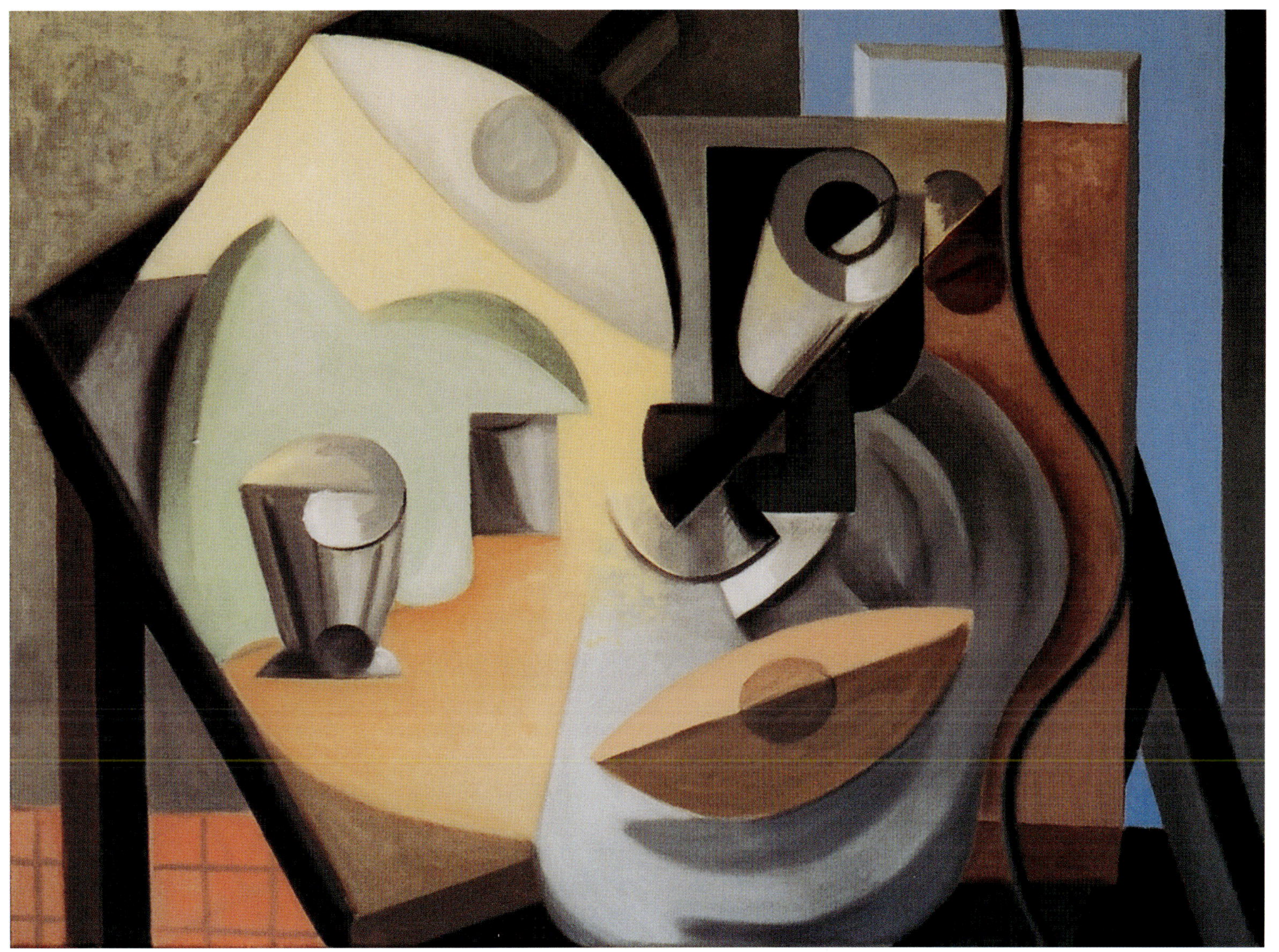

Lamp and Wire, 1989 Oil on board, 22" × 30"

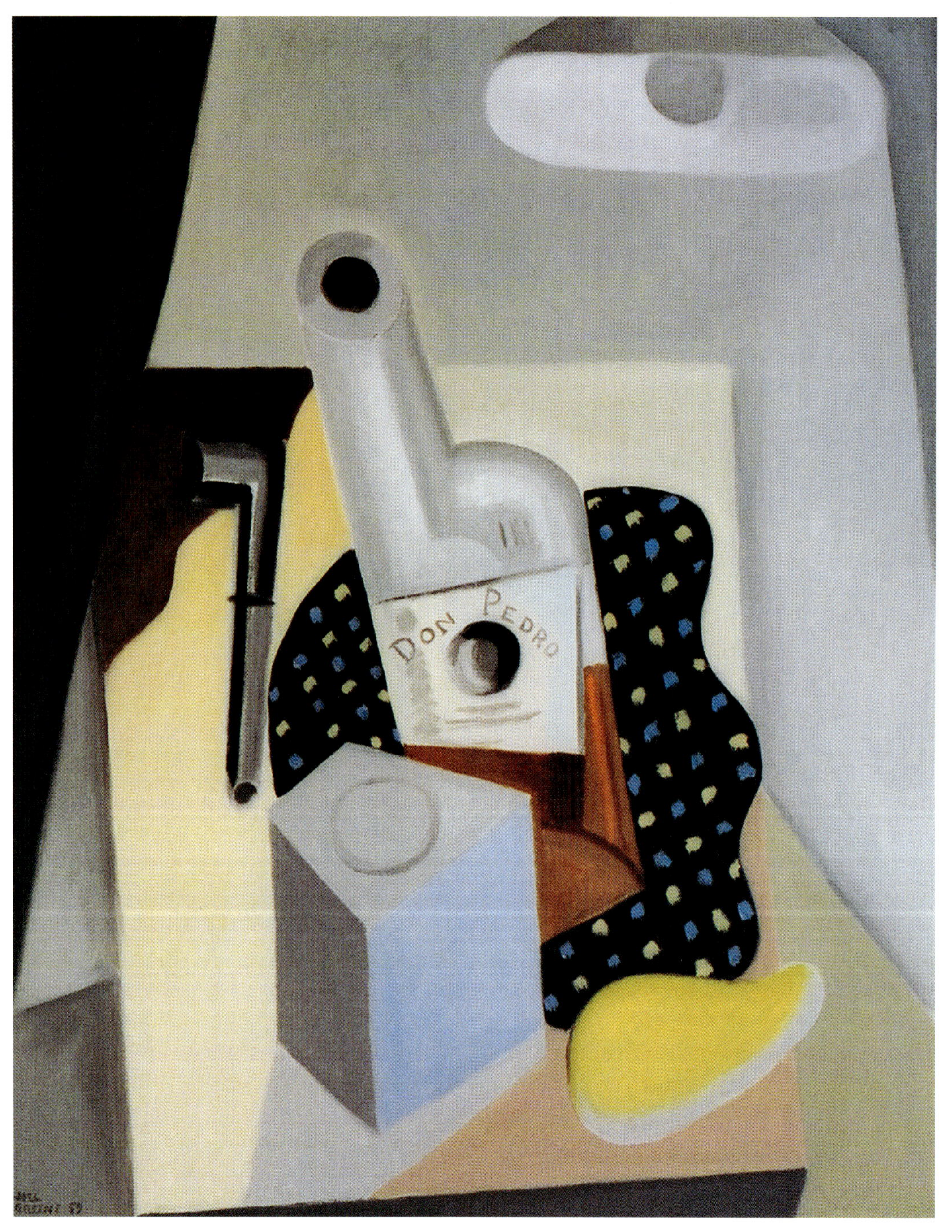

Don Pedro, 1989
Oil on linen, 20" × 16"

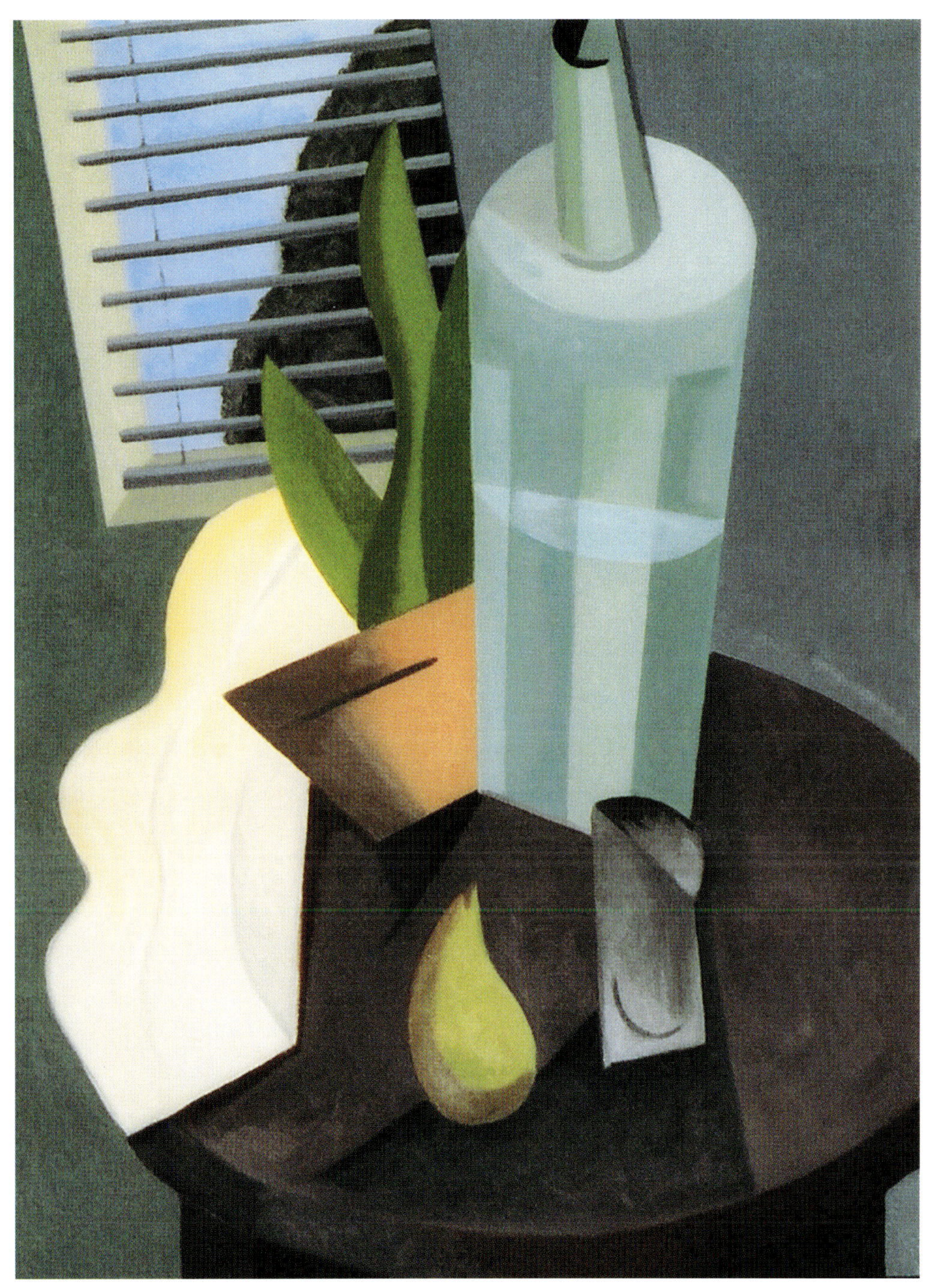

Fluted Bottle and Plant, 1994
Oil on linen, 18" × 24"

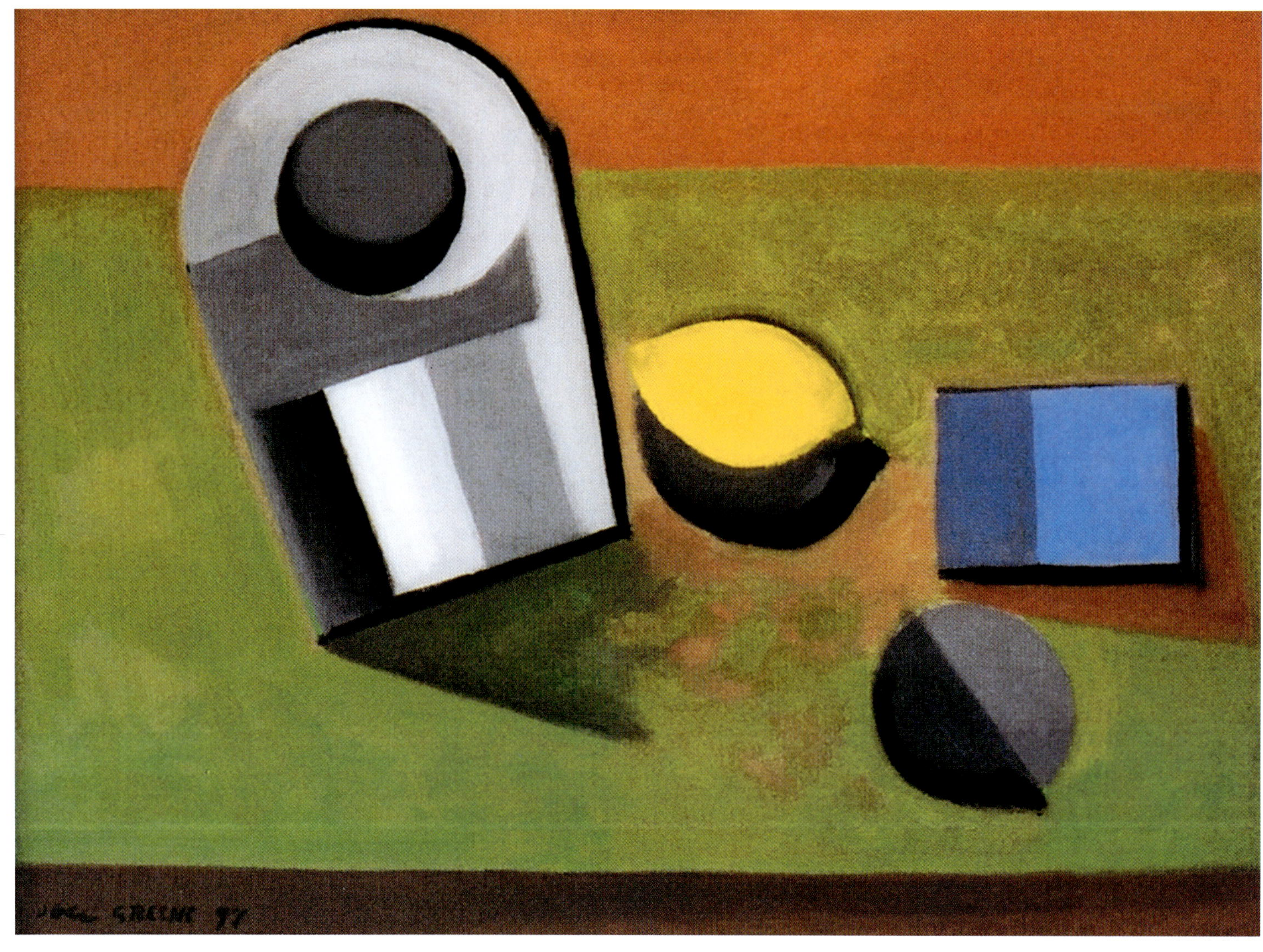

Glass, Cube and Fruit, 1997 — Oil on board, 7 ½" × 10 ⅜"

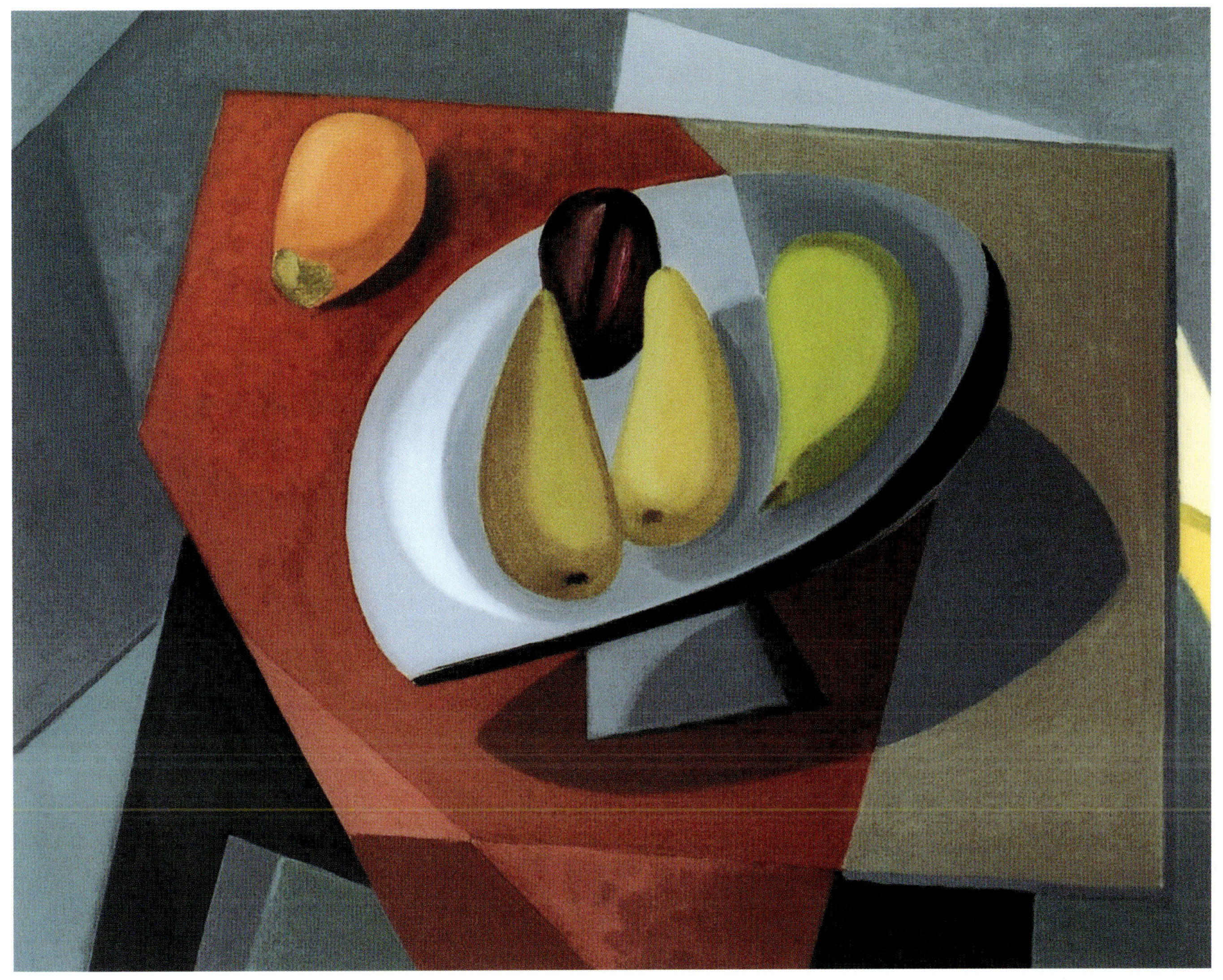

Persimmon, 1996 Oil on board, 16" × 20"

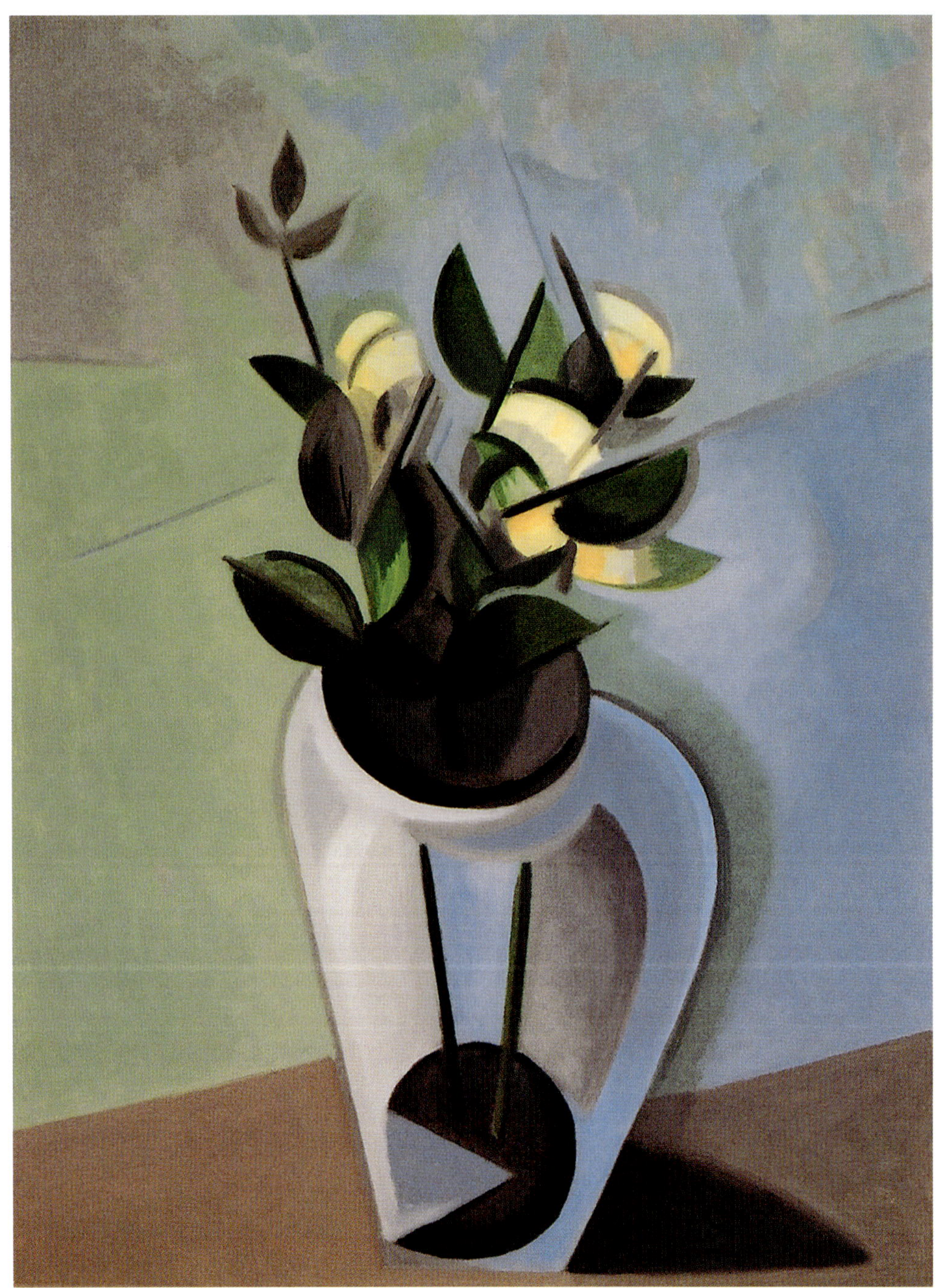

Roses, 1998
Oil on board, 16" × 12"

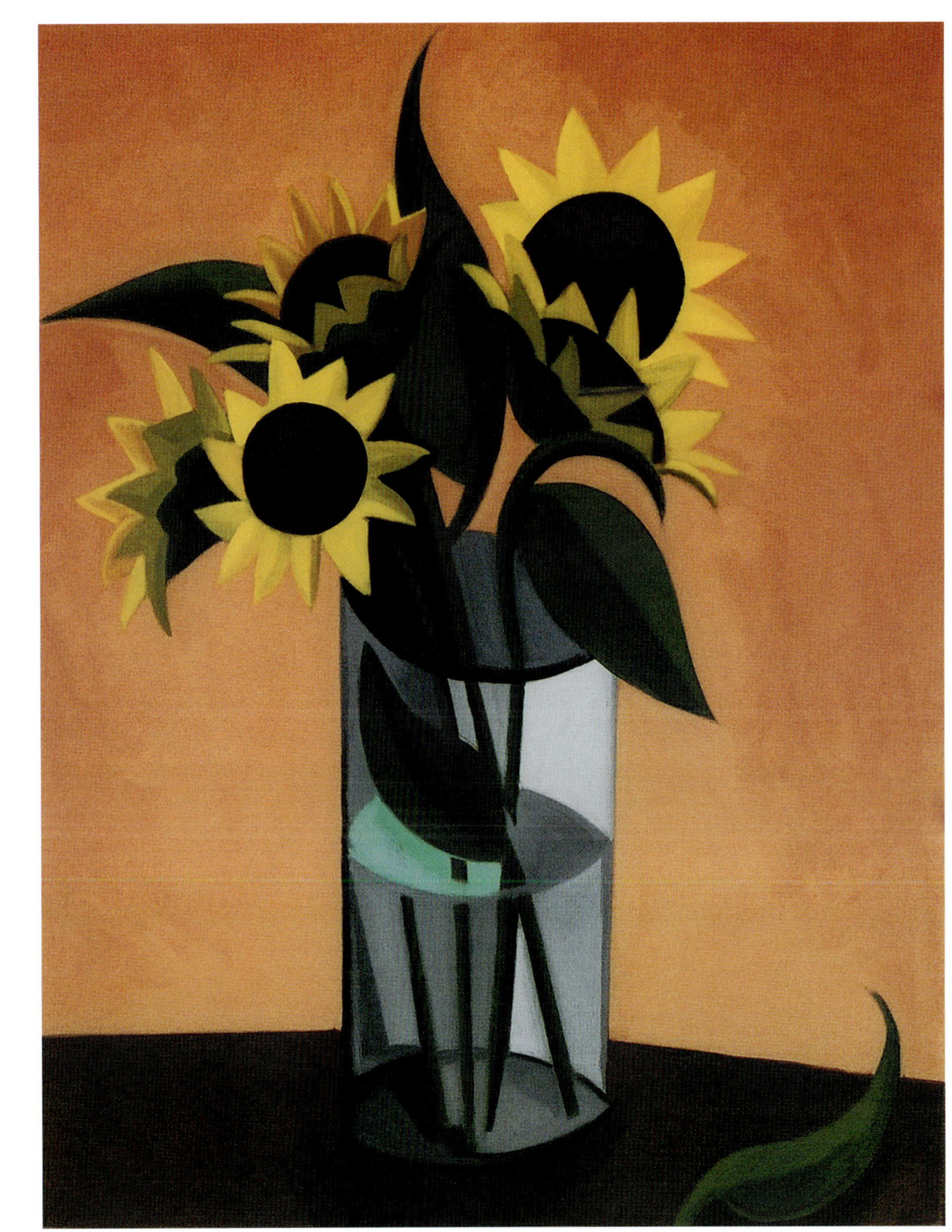

Sunflowers, 1997
Oil on board, 18" × 14"

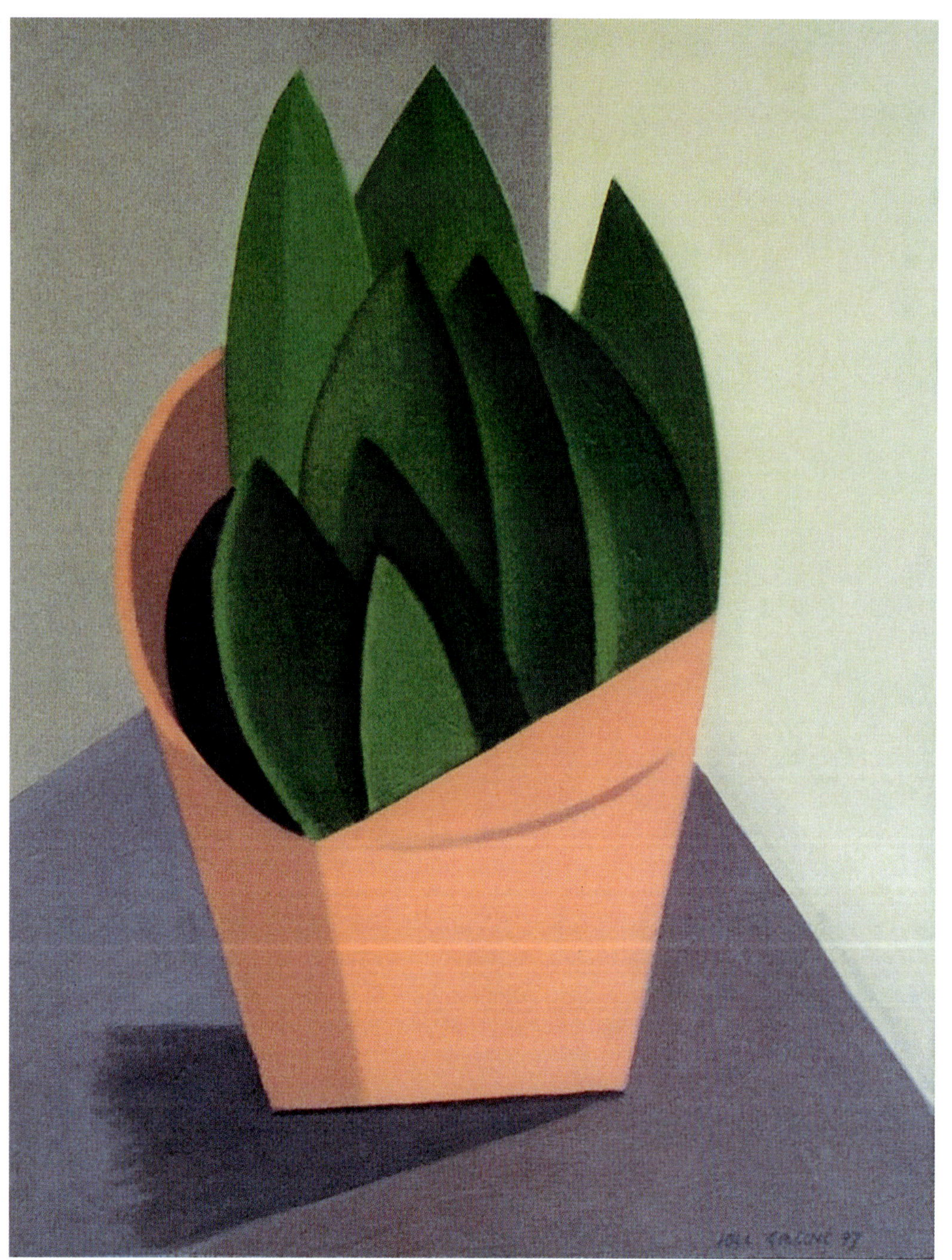

Plant, 1997

Oil on board, 14" × 11"

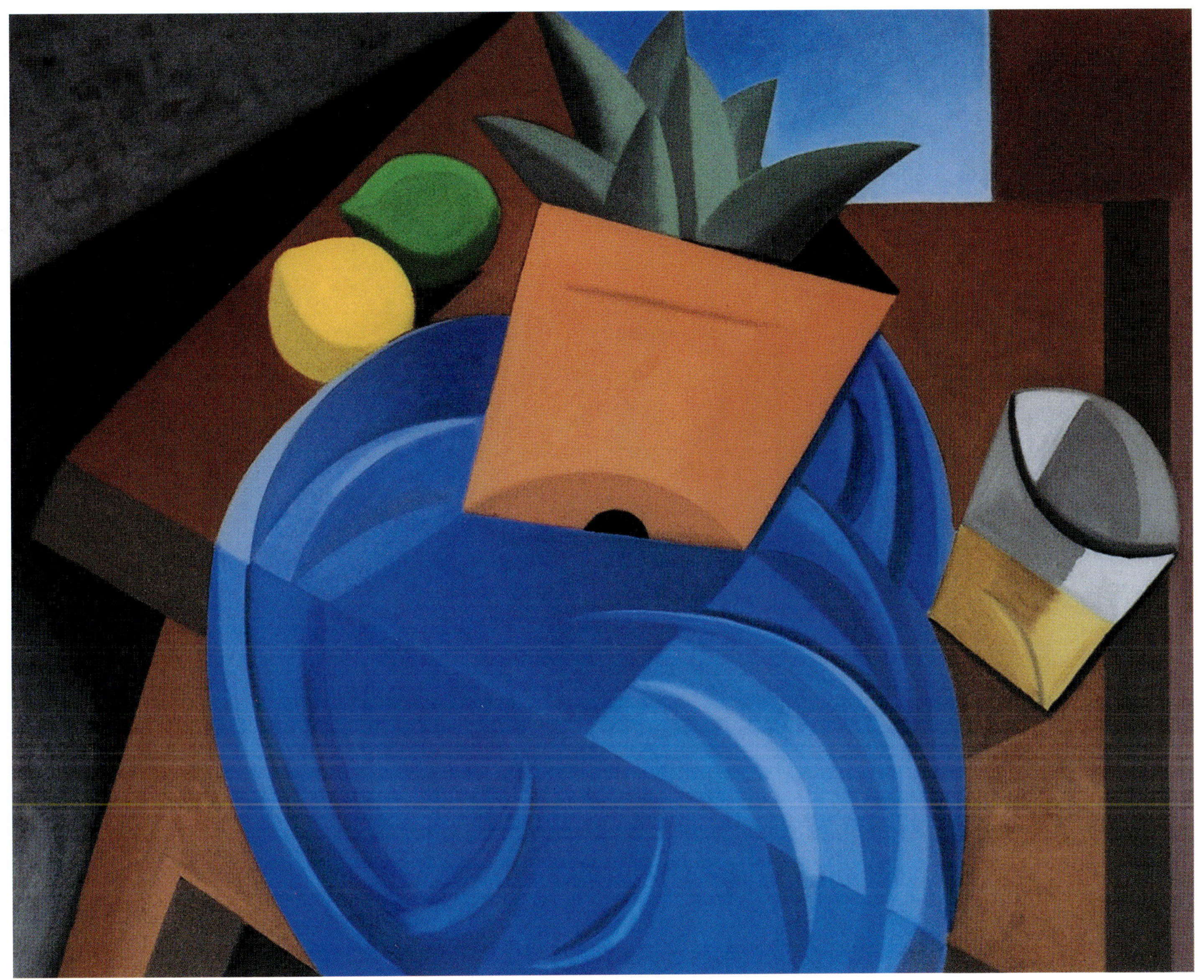

Plant, Blue Cloth and Window, 1997

Oil on linen, 16" × 20"

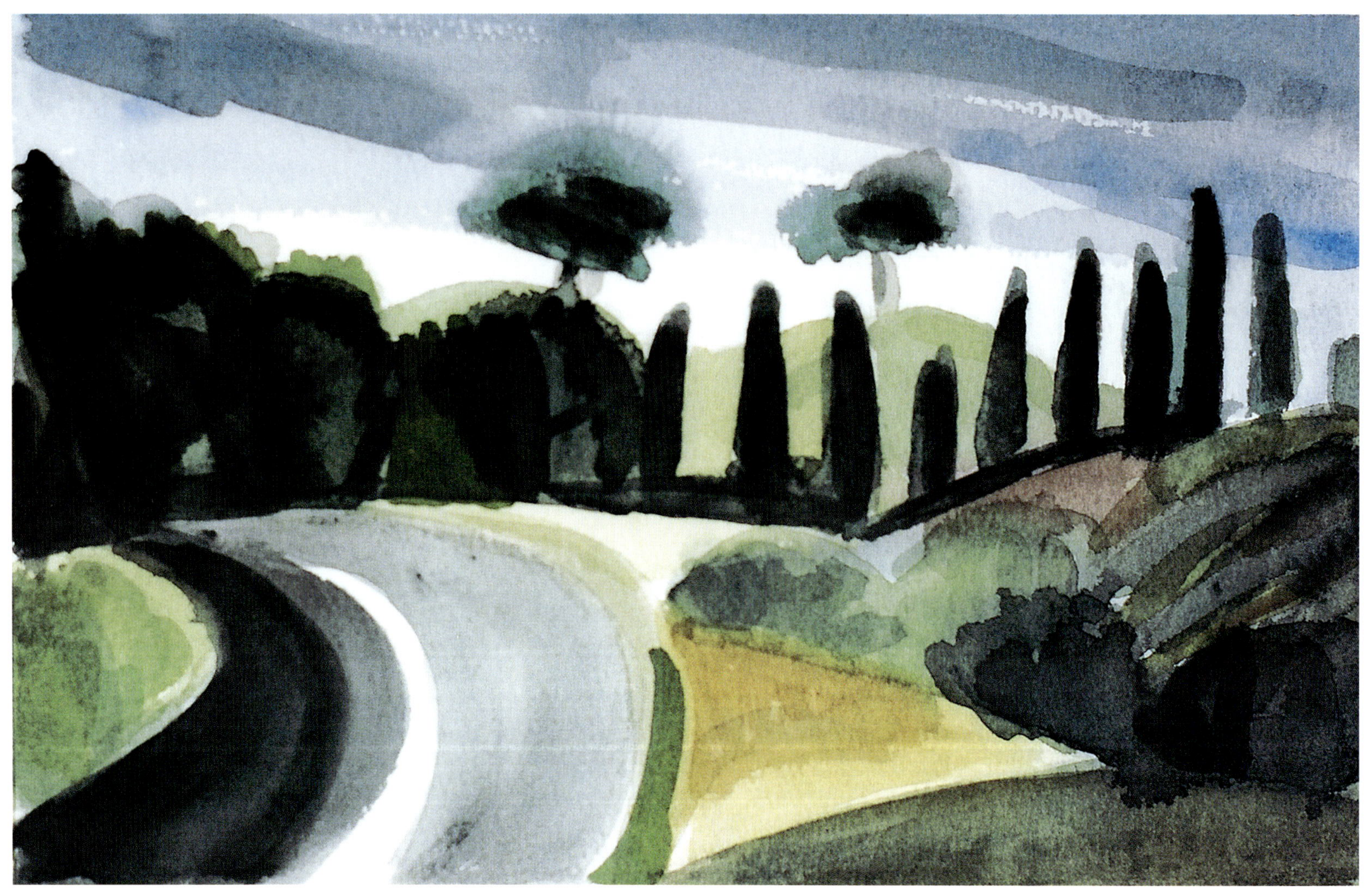

Tuscan Landscape, 1998 Watercolor, 6 ½" × 10 ¼"

tuscany: a transforming vision

It's such a beautiful place, but you realize everything's been touched by the hand of man, because people have been living there essentially forever. —Joel Greene

Joel's first visit to Tuscany in the summer of 1998 came at a propitious time in his career and ushered in an important shift in his style. After playing with a Cubist-inspired perspective in still life, and to some extent in his early landscapes, he was ready for new artistic ground to explore. "I'll do one kind of work for a year or two, or longer, until I feel like I've wrung it out," he notes. "Then I'll move into something else. I don't want to become formulaic."

Thus, in the receptive spirit of a transitional phase in his art, he accepted a friend's invitation to join a group of a dozen travelers on a two-week Italian sojourn. Home base was a spacious villa in a wooded valley near Montalcino. While the others slept late, Joel happily greeted Tuscan mornings on the villa's porch with his coffee and pipe, and then he set off with the group each day to explore new sights. Traveling light, he took only a sketchbook and pencils. He also shot several rolls of film.

The Tuscany photos, it turns out, played a key role in what Joel considers a breakthrough in his work. Previously he had avoided the camera as a painting tool; now he reconsidered that choice. Back home in his studio, he pulled out images that interested him most and began to paint, first in watercolor, soon shifting to oils. As with all his art, the scene before his eyes, captured now in a photo, was simply a starting place. The rolling hills and patchwork farms punctuated by rows of cypress trees, the winding country roads and the ancient, red-roofed towns were all raw material for the puzzle of interlocking shapes and color with which he loves to play.

But with Tuscany his work took a conscious step toward a more naturalistic look. Although still abstracted in a stylized vocabulary of shapes, the imagery shed its more angular, rigidly geometric notes. Instead, it began to dance with a fluid, lyrical rhythm that emphasized volume and curves. At the same time, Joel maintained his interest in a quiet, even light and compressed sense of space. "It took off for me. It was very exciting. I used the Tuscany material for an entire year," he recounts. And soon, it would color his dialogue with the New Mexico landscape and sky as well.

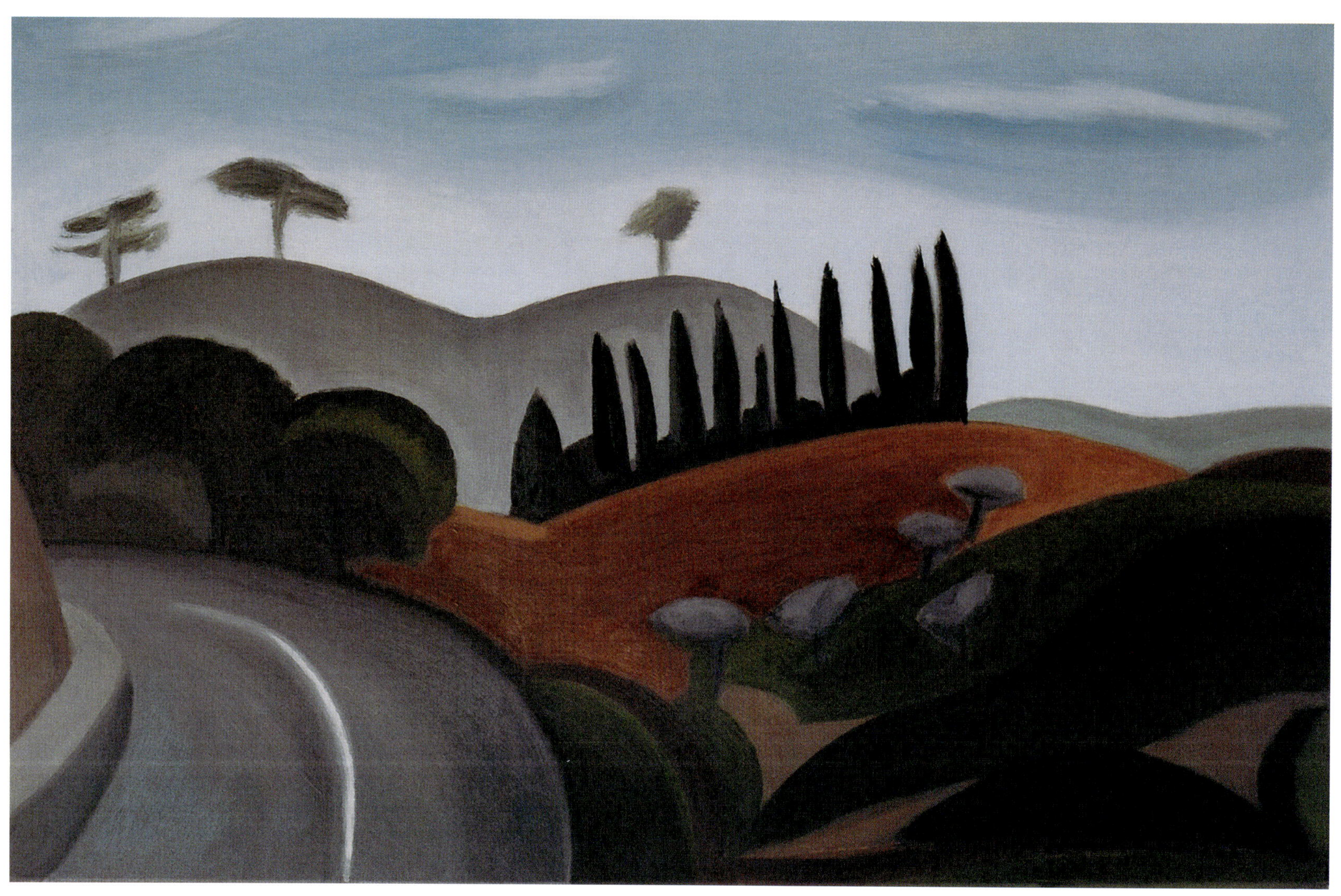

Tuscany Hilltop Trees, 1998 Oil on board, 7" × 11"

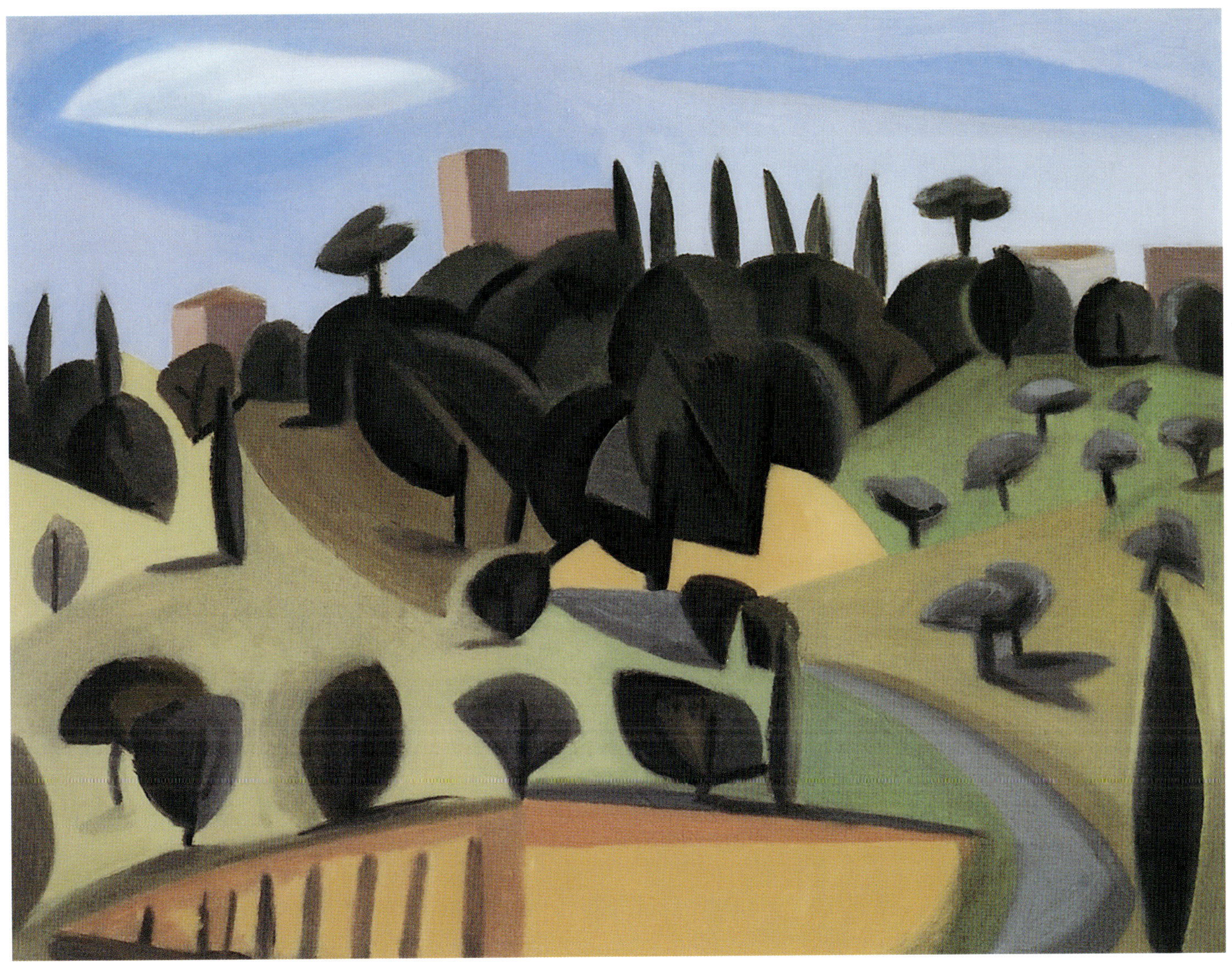

Tuscany Chianti Castle, 1998

Oil on board, 9" × 12"

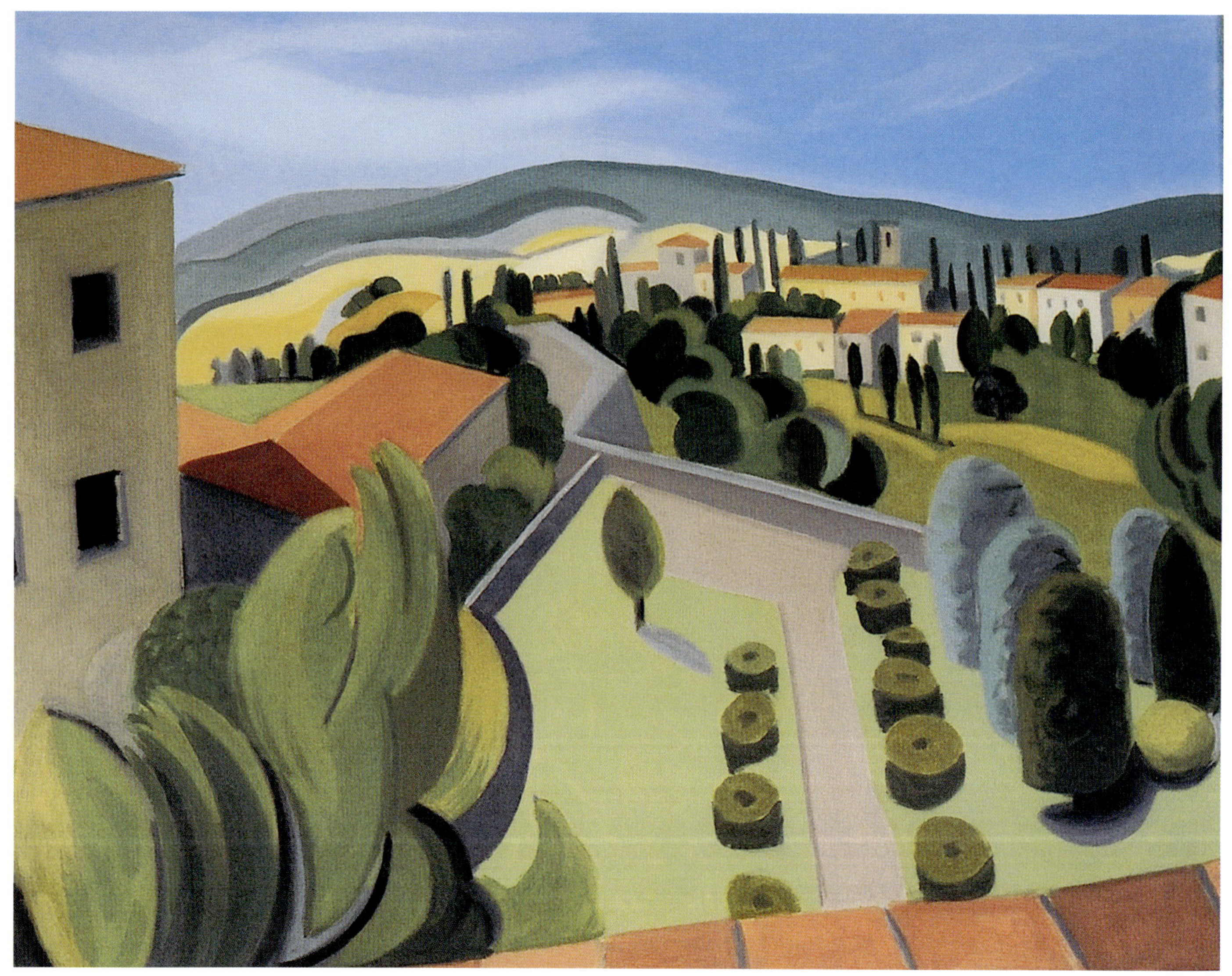

Topiary Garden Volterra, 1999

Oil on board, 14" × 18"

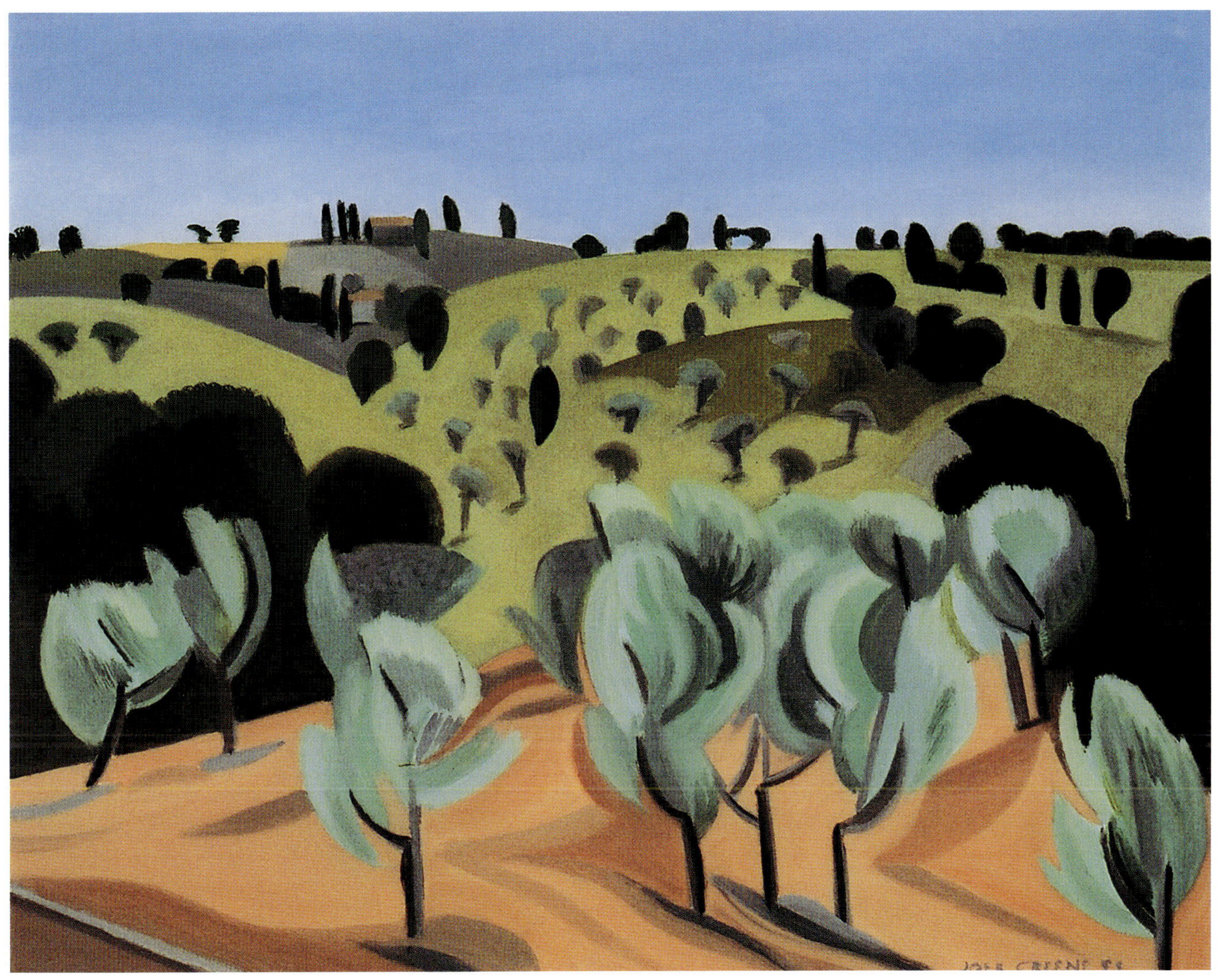

Olive Grove, 1999

Oil on board, 11" × 14"

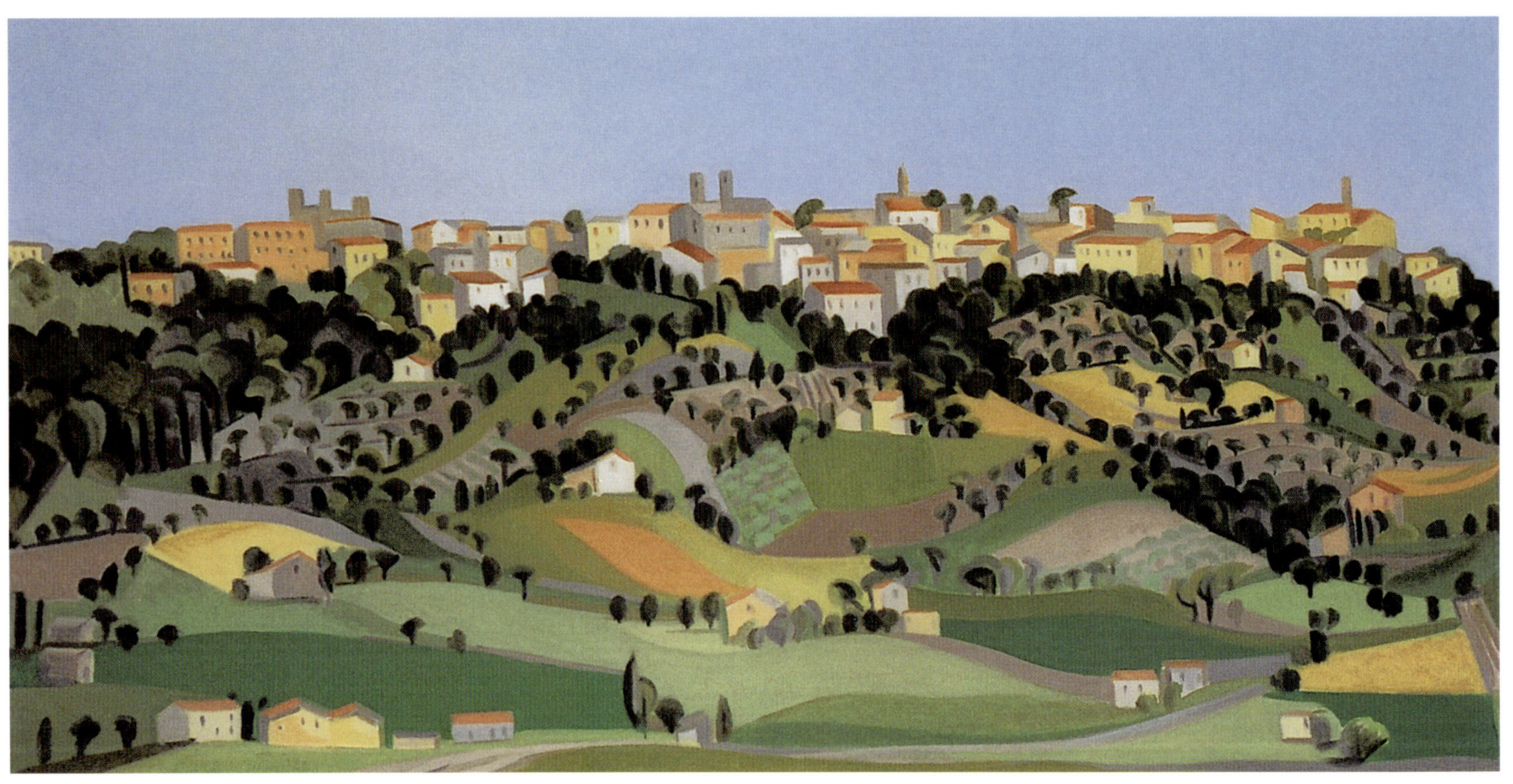

Montalcino, 1999 Oil on linen, 16" × 32"

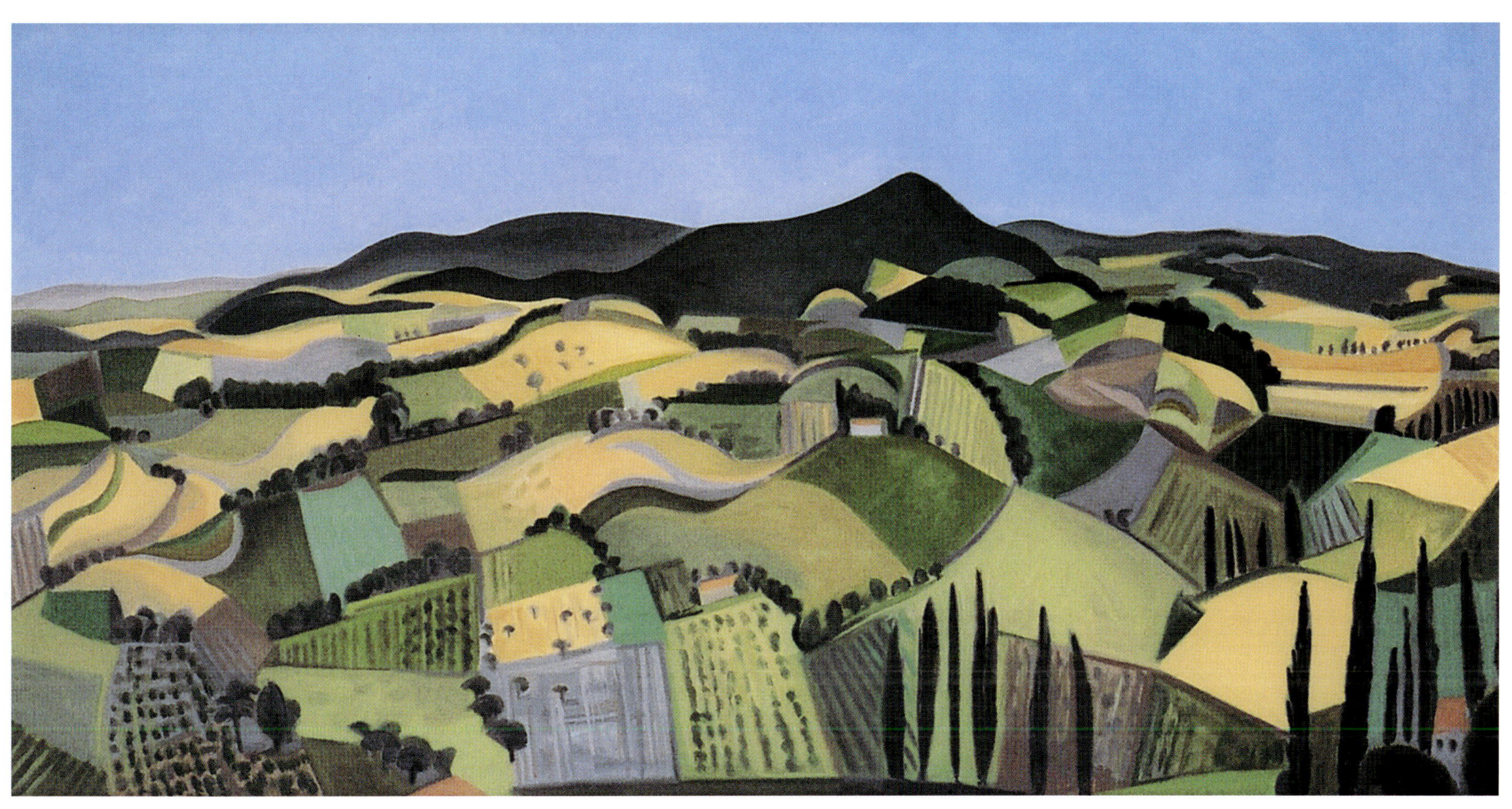

Pienza, 1998 Oil on linen, 16" × 32"

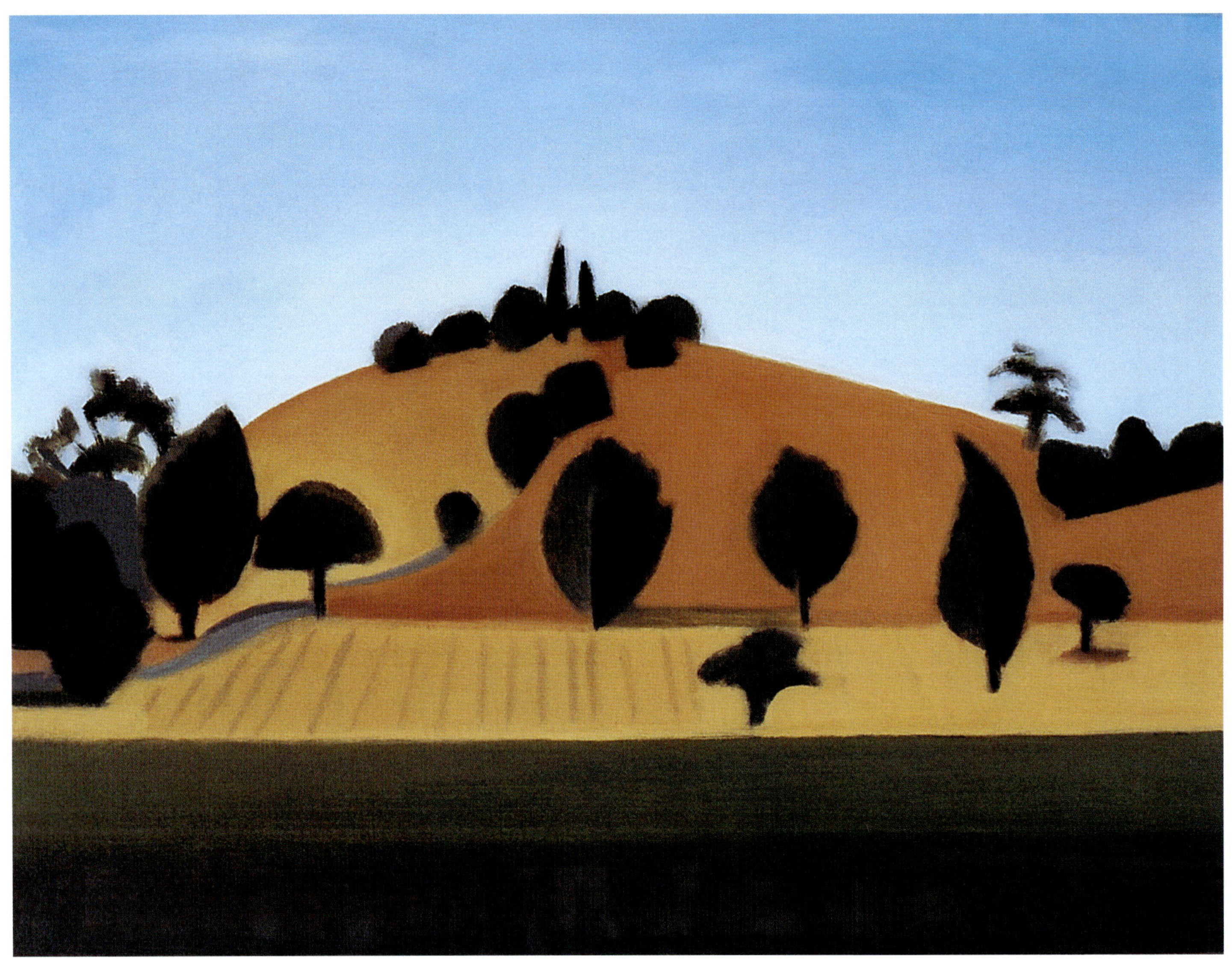

Tuscany Trees and Fields, 1998

Oil on board, 8 ¾" × 10 ¾"

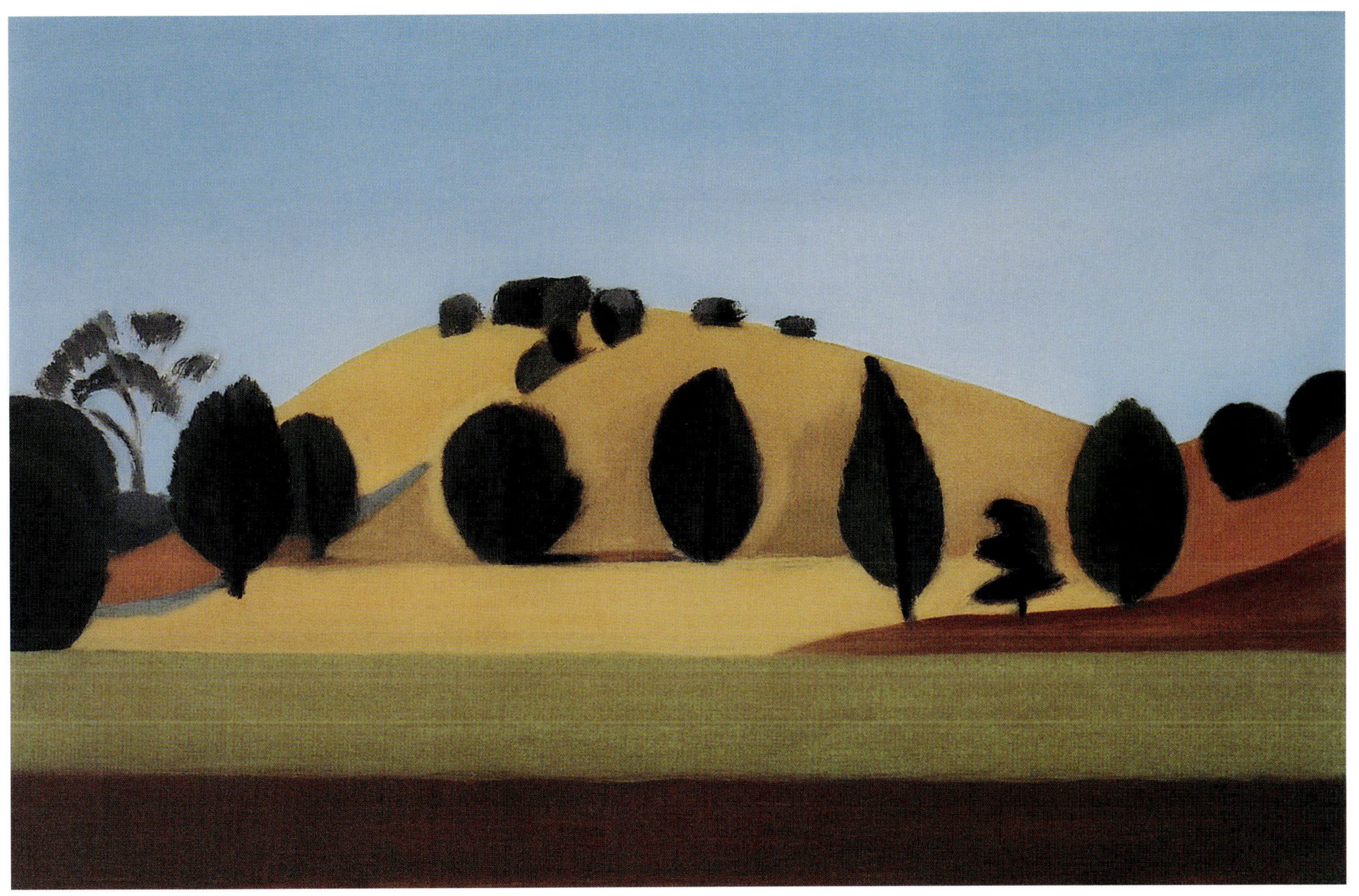

Tuscany Trees and Fields, 1998

Oil on board, 7" × 11"

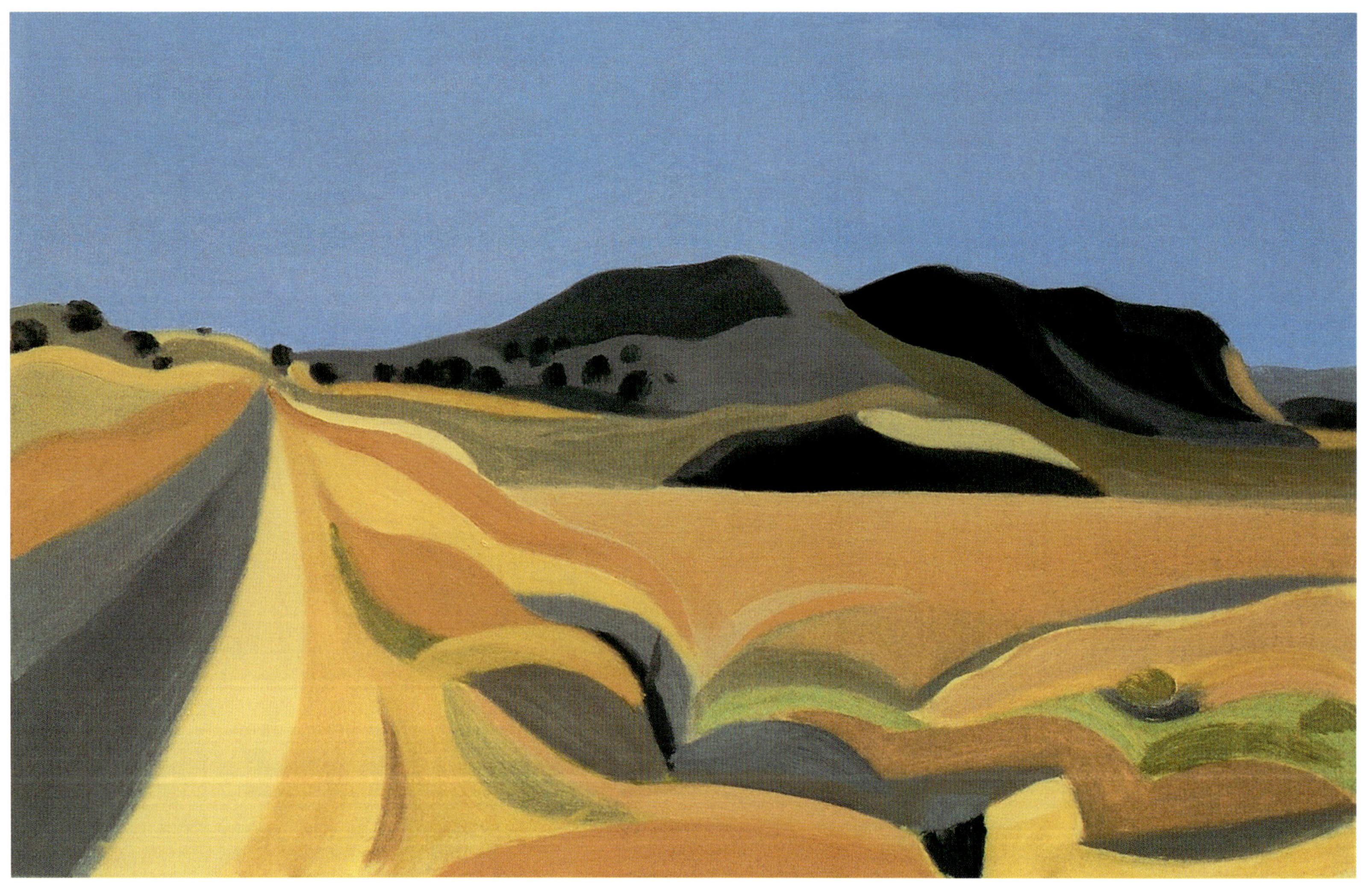

Road With Black Hills, 2000 Oil on board, 7" × 11"

essential new mexico: recent works

Getting over the idea that I couldn't use photos allowed me to put the top down on the Miata and go for a nice drive and call myself working. —Joel Greene

After Tuscany, as Joel turned his attention once more to the New Mexico landscape, his use of the camera had effectively turned a page in his art. His earlier reliance on memory and imagination now was enriched by the use of the photograph as a springboard for composition and design. It served to animate in the artist a new level of response to a scene, and he began to translate the vocabulary of land and sky through the sinuous syntax of curving shapes.

The Swiss surrealist painter and sculptor Alberto Giacometti once proposed that "the object of art is not to reproduce reality, but to create a reality of the same intensity." Some landscape painters attempt to convey the intensity of the West through dramatic contrasts of light and dark or in highly detailed renderings. For Joel, the truth of what he sees is expressed as movement and flow. In this way his art gives form to the unseen elements of geologic time and the invisible but endlessly carving forces of water and wind on the high desert land. This honesty of vision, as one collector put it, is at the heart of Joel's work.

To gather material, the artist often roams New Mexico's roadways, stopping, for example, at a site overlooking the sweep of juniper-dotted grasslands near Galisteo Dam, south of Santa Fe at the base of La Bajada. In his paintings of this area one senses the prehistoric rolling ocean floor this land once was. Other favorite Miata rides include a winding country road along the Pecos River toward the village of Villanueva, between Santa Fe and Joel's boyhood home of Las Vegas. Or he'll head north to the commanding, striated red rock cliffs near Abiquiú, much depicted and beloved by Georgia O'Keeffe.

Because his paintings don't focus on naturalistic lighting, Joel has no need to photograph at certain times of the day. In fact, he says with a smile, lousy photos provide his best material. "Then I can't get too fussy about all the little details and lose track of the whole thing. I'm more interested in balancing the weight, forms, colors, directions, the way the eye moves through the picture. It shares a lot with music. A dynamic composition is all about building those visual tensions and rhythms and balancing all the elements—that's what makes painting satisfying to me."

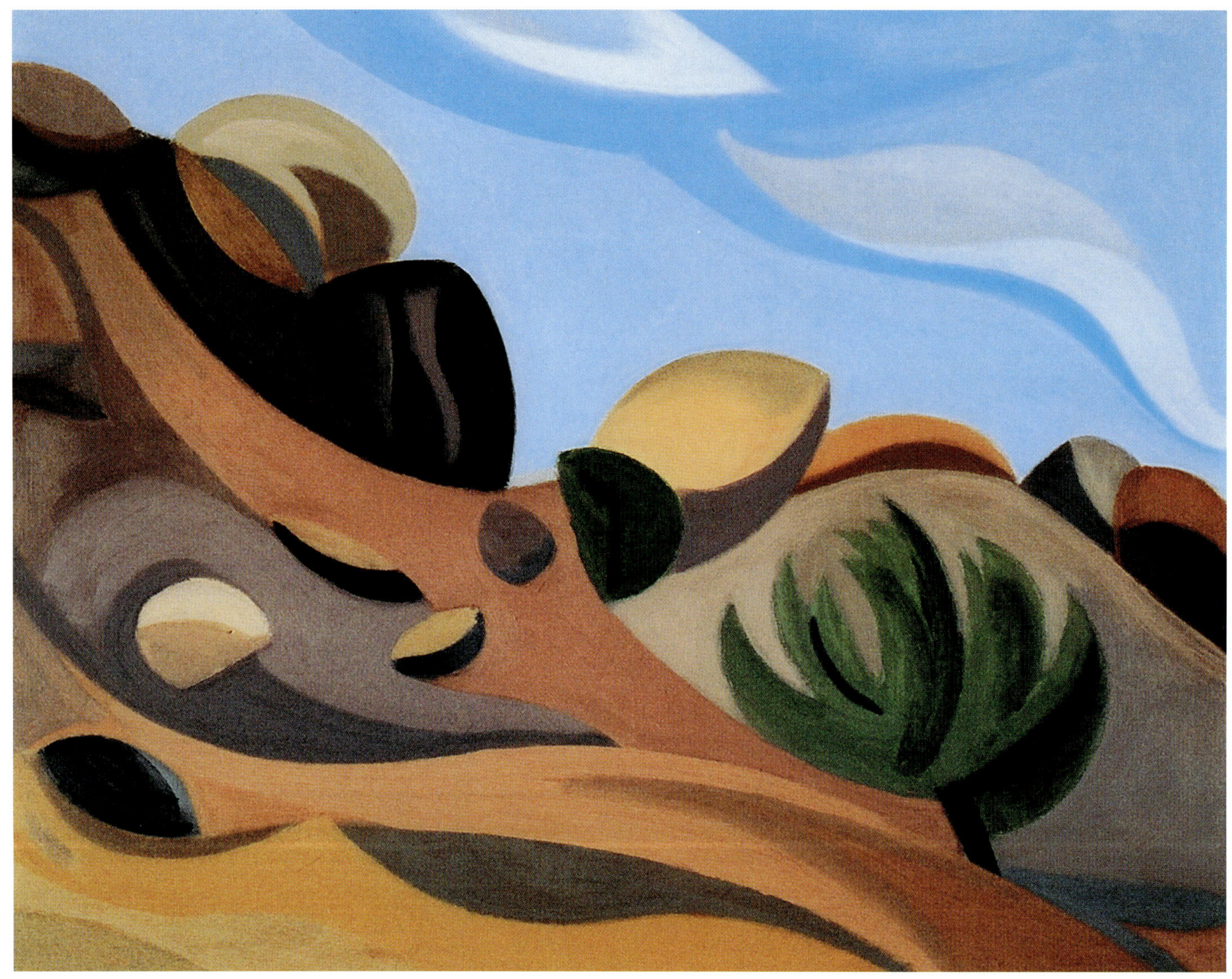

Boulders, Red Rocks, 2003 | Oil on board, 11" × 14"

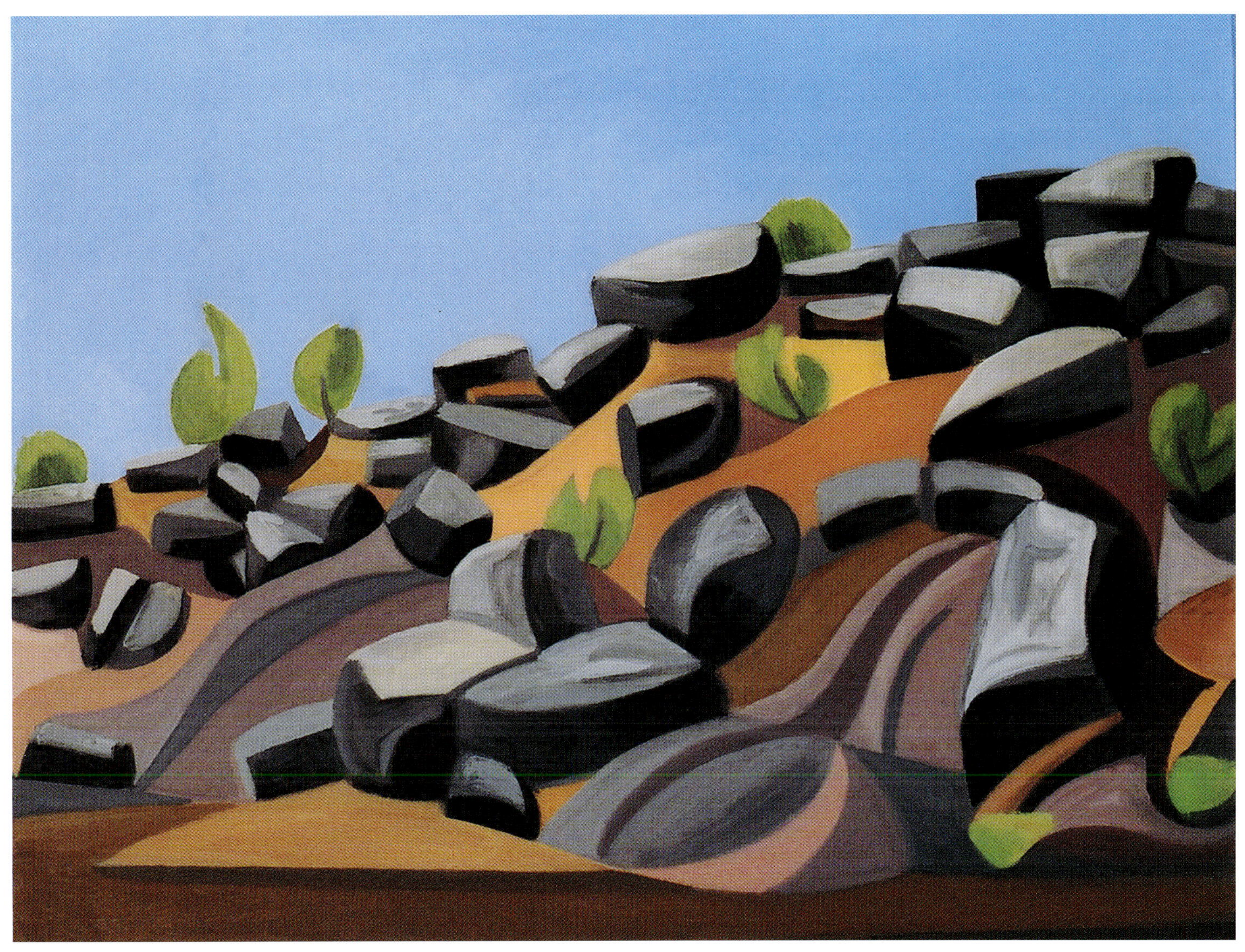

Road Cut Near Ribera, 2000 Oil on board, 12" × 16"

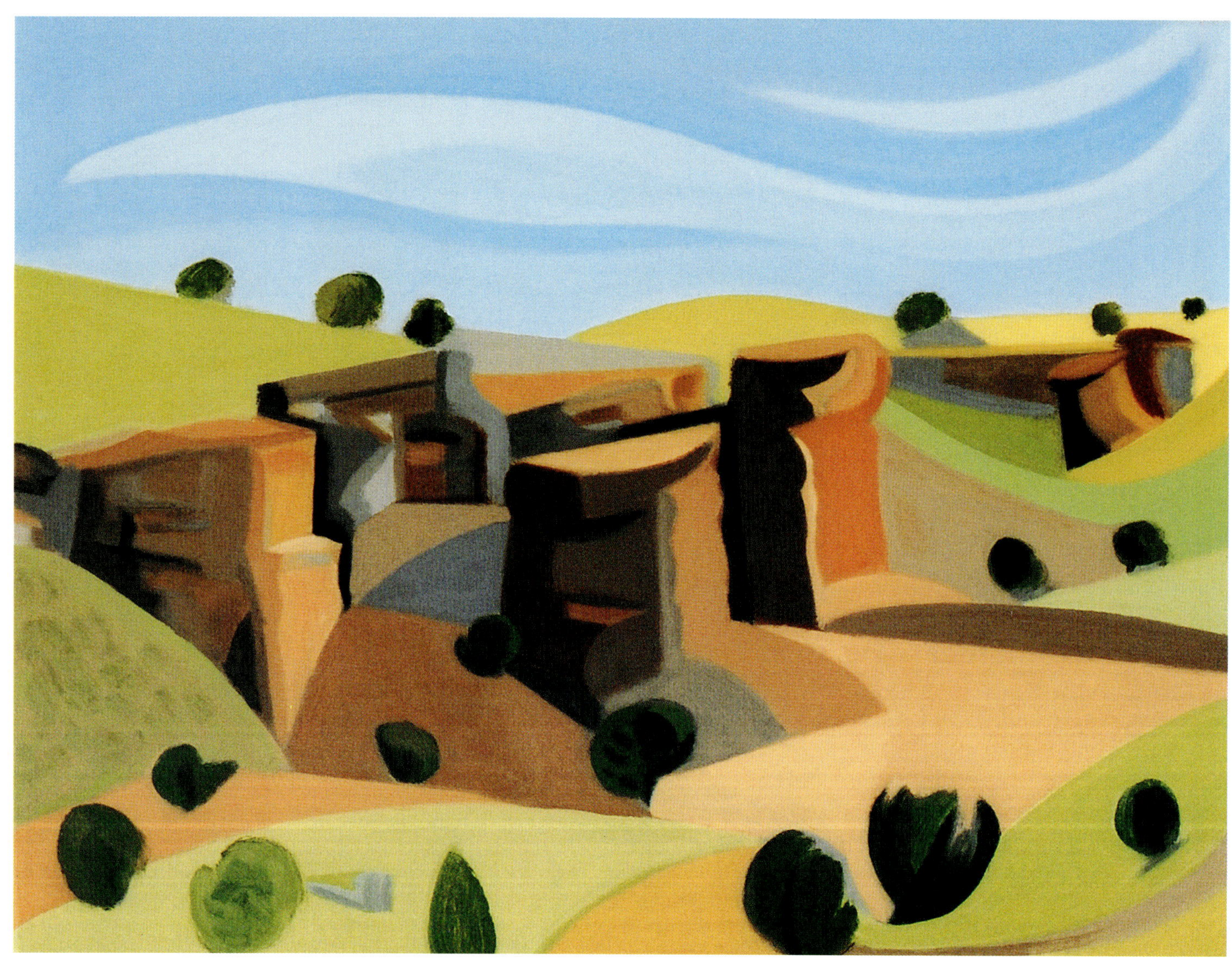

Rock Formations Near Cundiyó, 2001

Oil on board, 9" × 12"

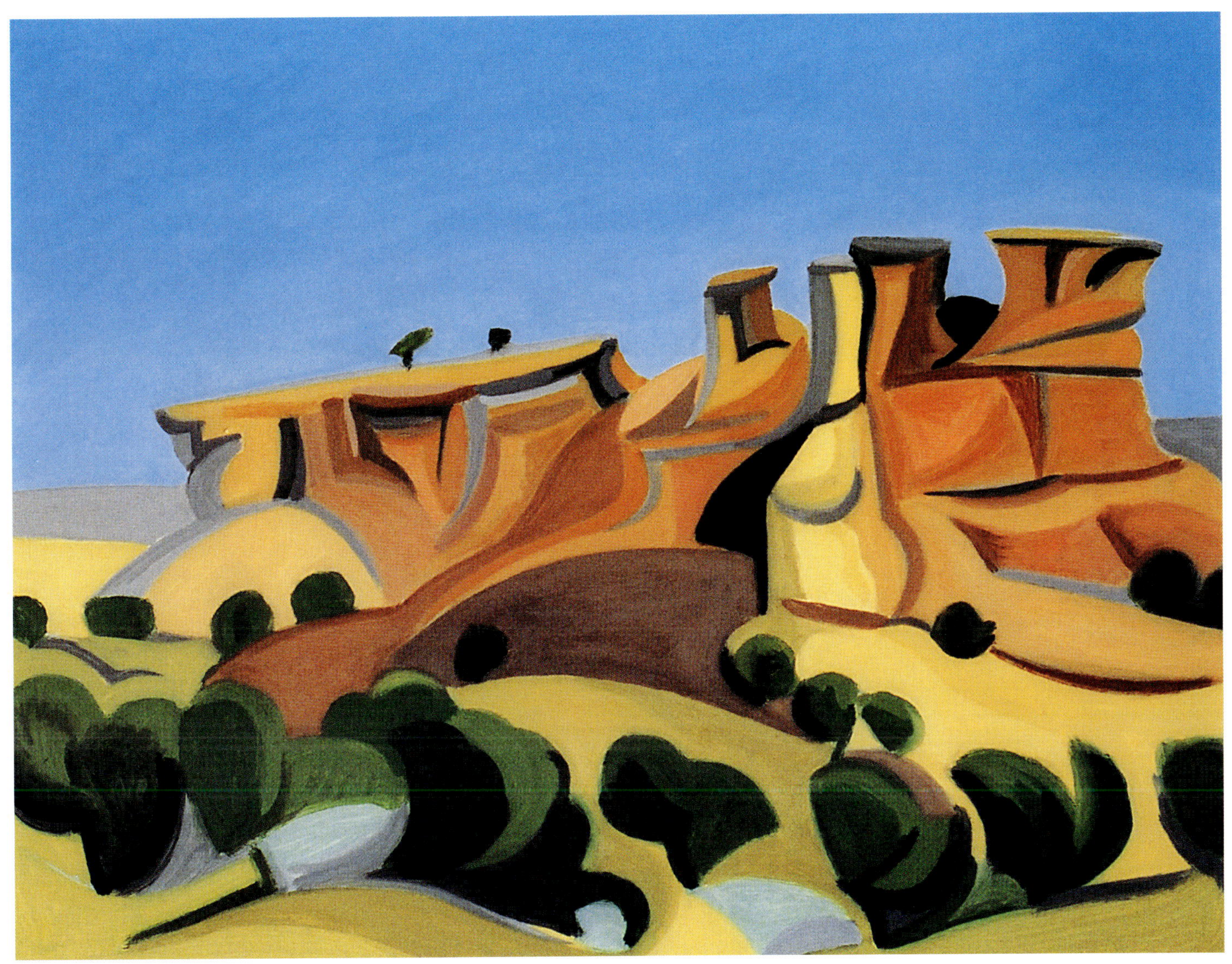

Rock Formations Near Cundiyó, 2000 Oil on board, 12" × 16"

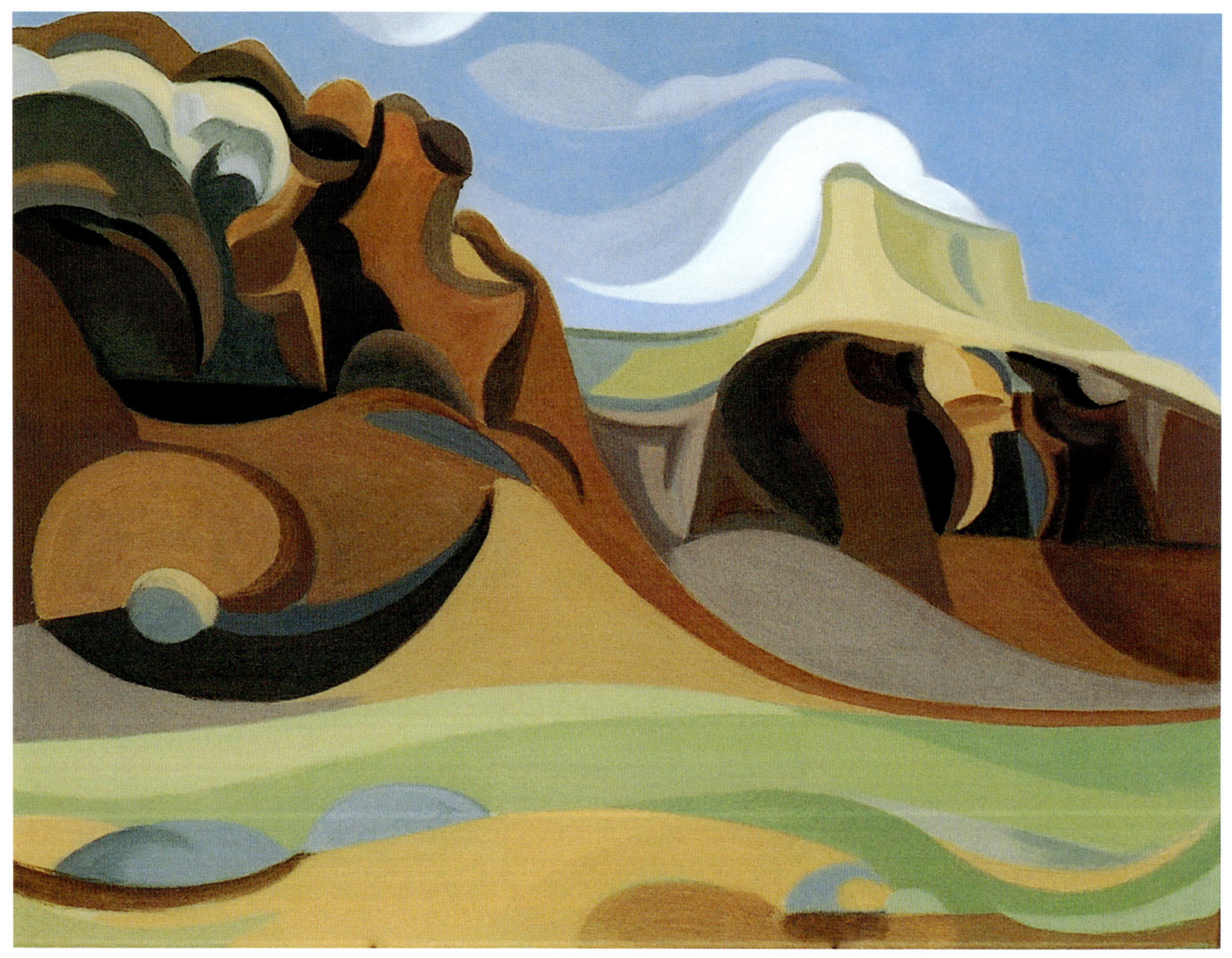

Red Rocks Abiquiú, 2003 Oil on board, 12" × 16"

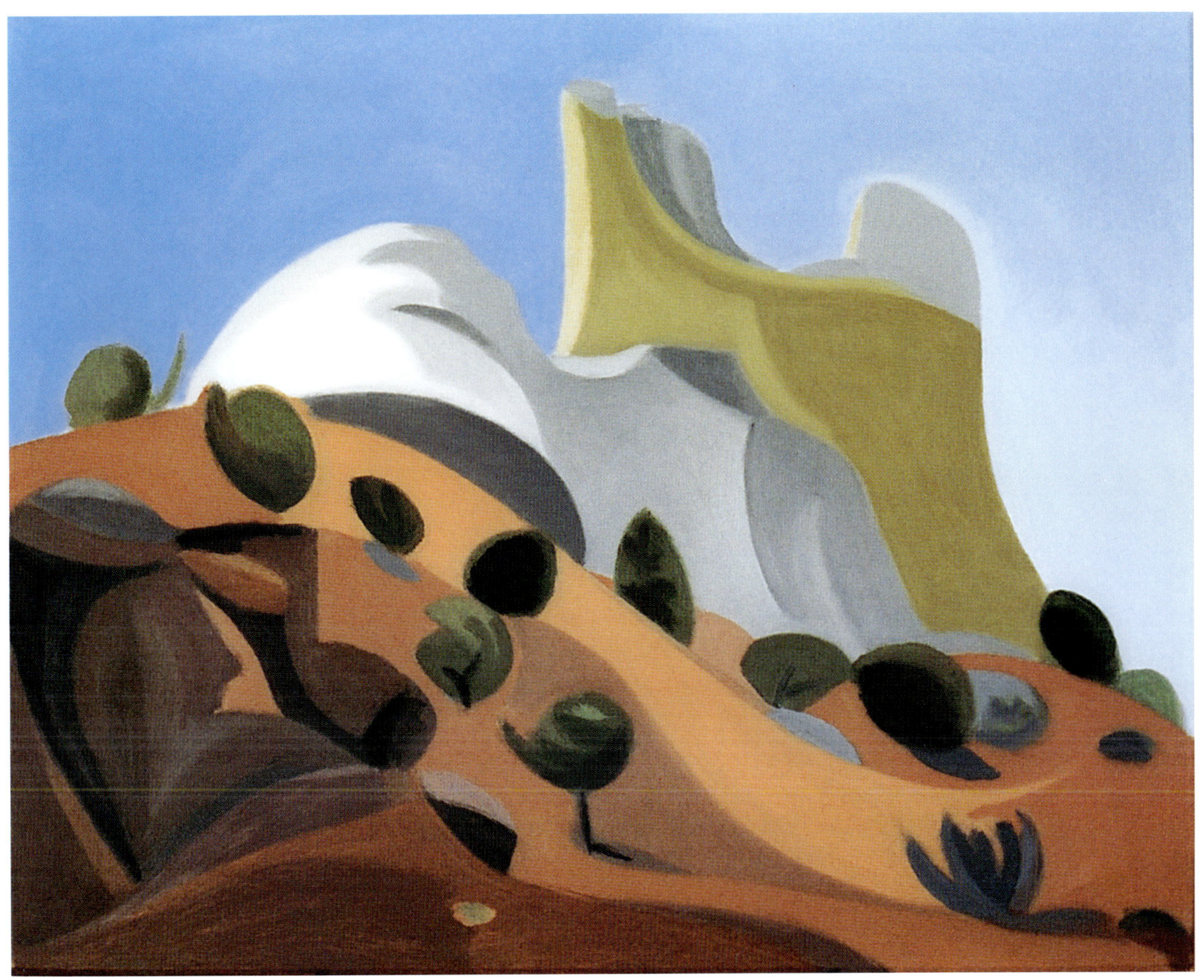

Near Echo Amphitheater, 2003 Oil on board, 11" × 14"

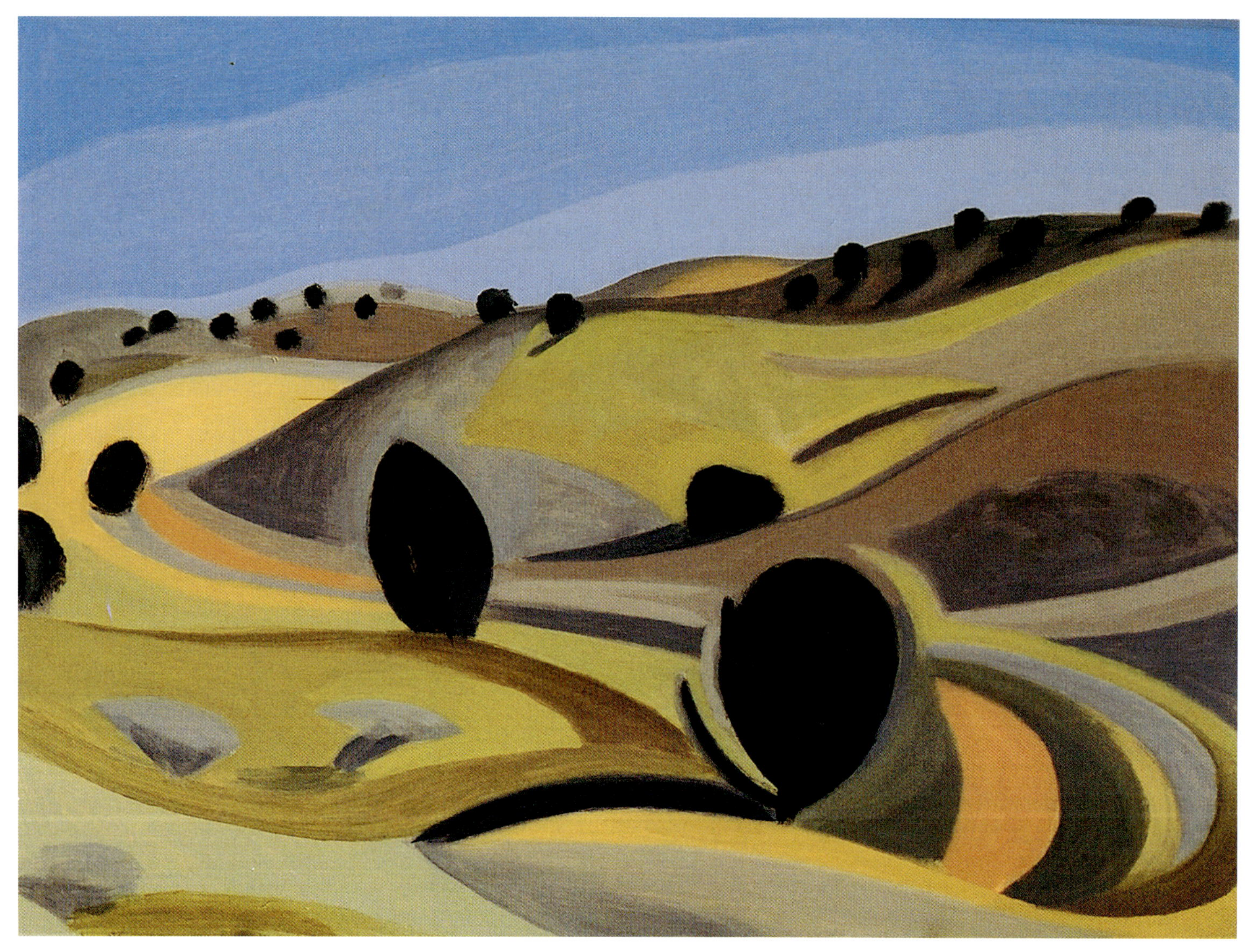

Near Peña Blanca, 2000 — Oil on board, 8" × 11"

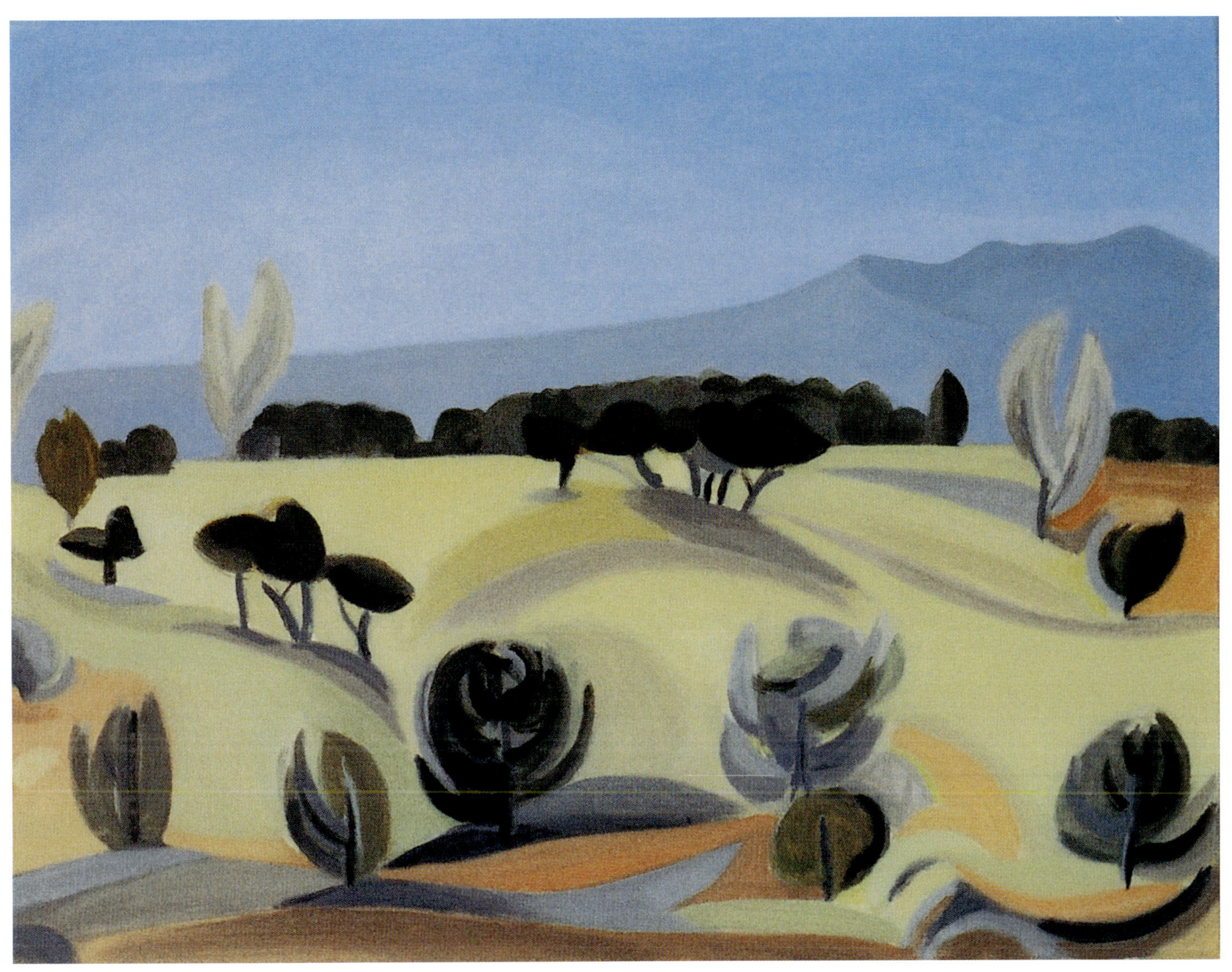

Nine Mile Road, 2000

Oil on board, 9" × 12"

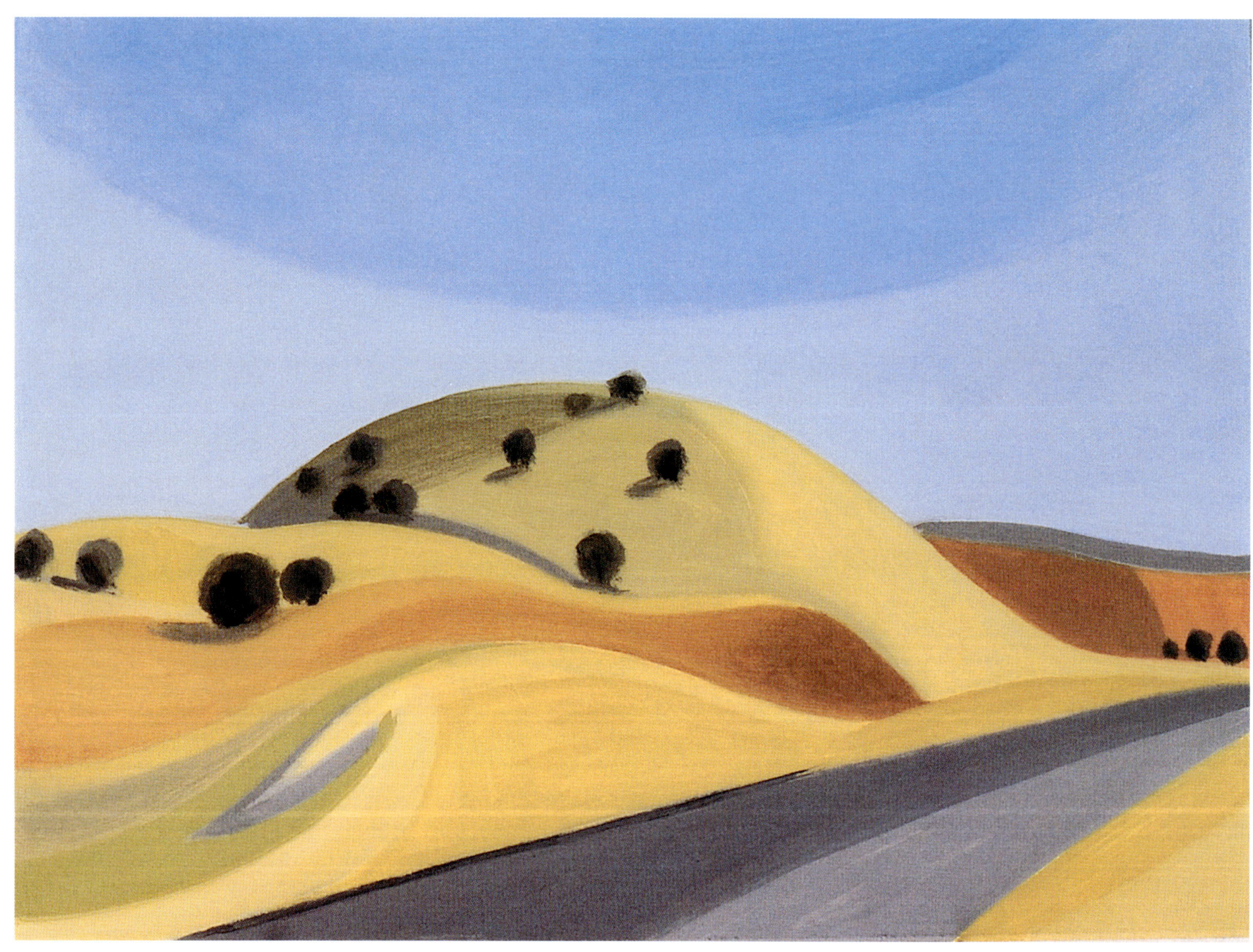

New Mexico Desert Landscape, 2001 Oil on board, 8" × 11"

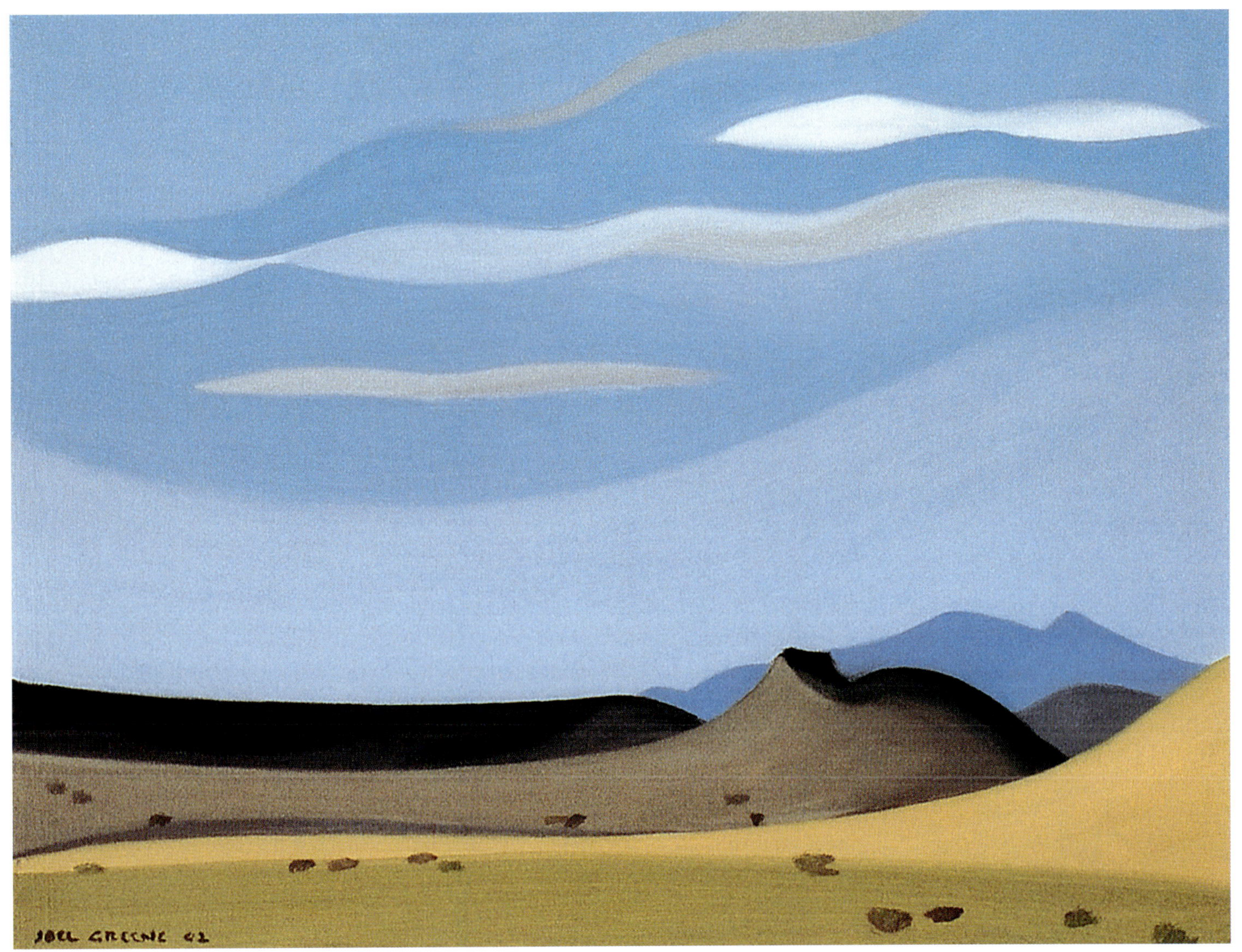

Hogbacks Highway 41, 2002

Oil on board, 9" × 12"

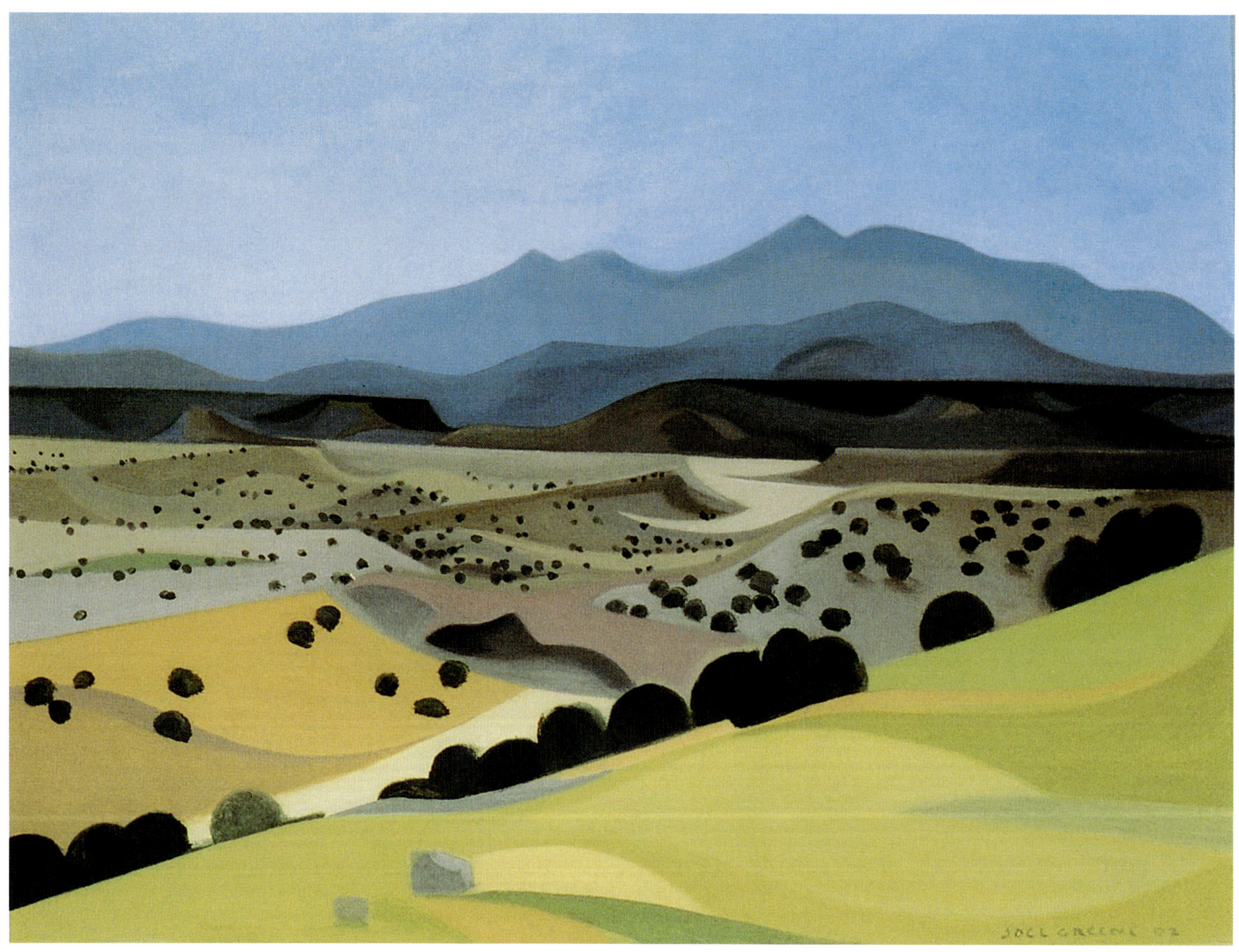

From Galisteo Dam East, 2002 Oil on board, 12" × 16"

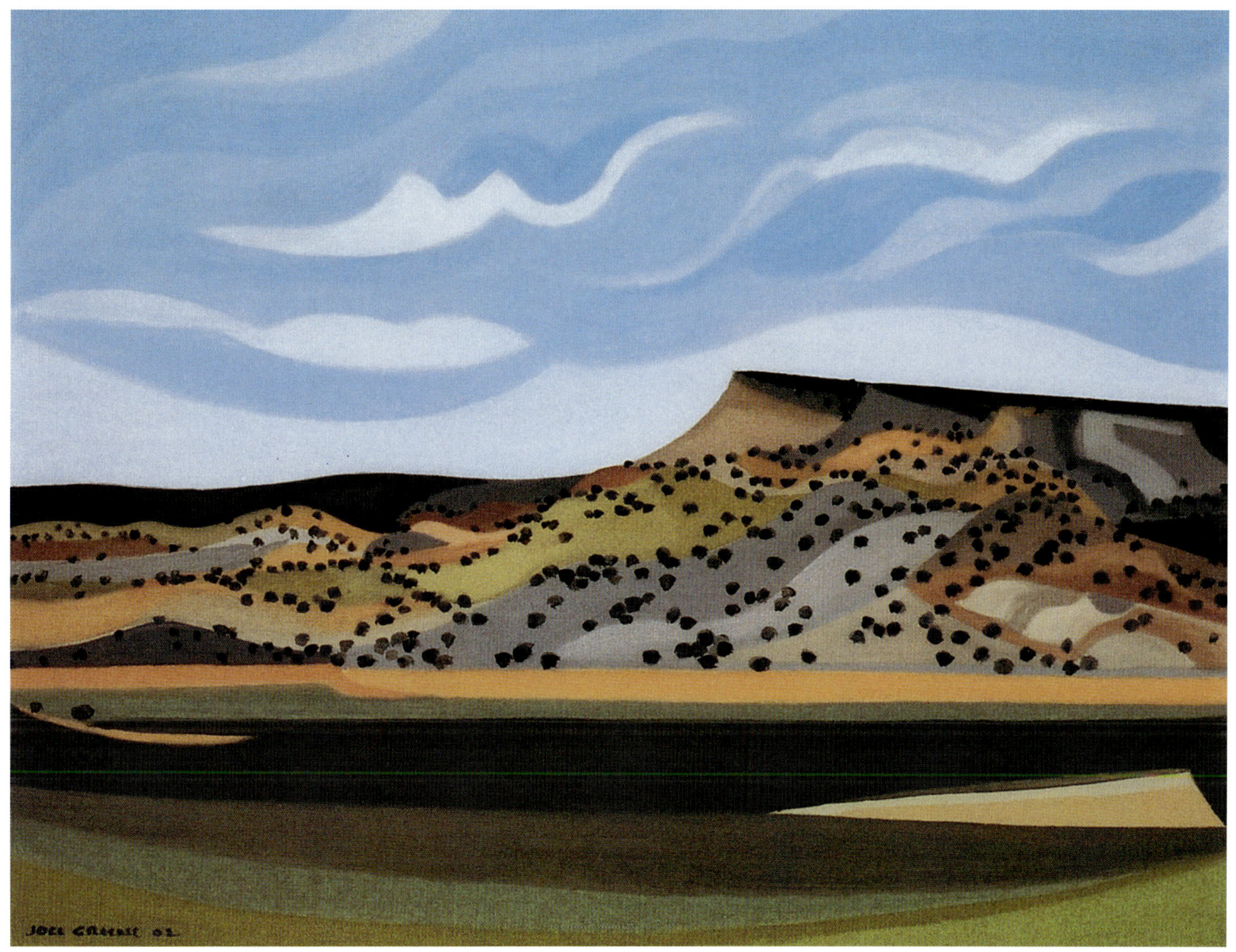

La Bajada, 2002

Oil on board, 12" × 16"

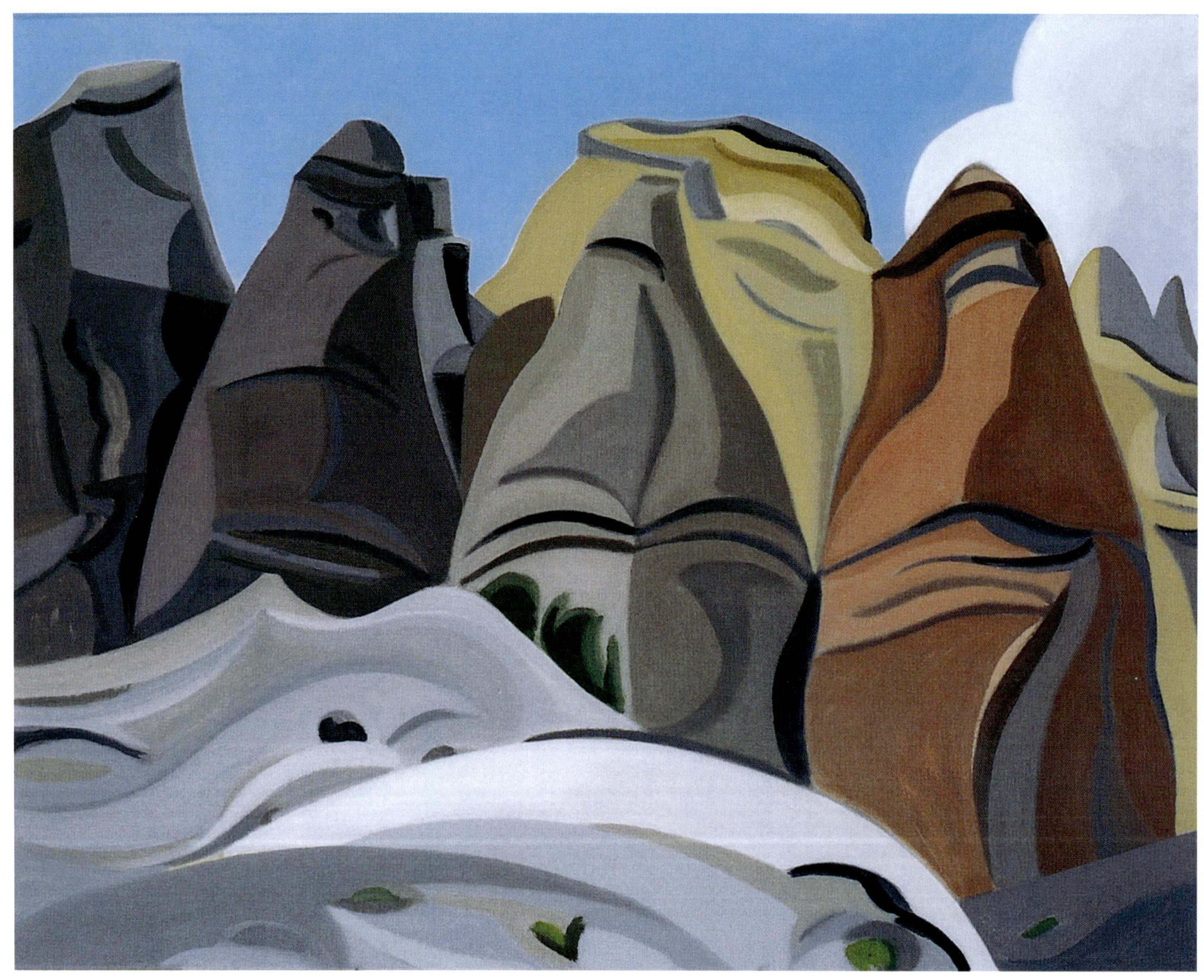

Tent Rocks, 2002 — Oil on board, 14" × 18"

tent rocks

It's like a fairyland—it's such a bizarre place. —Joel Greene

If there's one place that seems custom-made for Joel's artistic style, it is an area of extraordinary natural formations known as Tent Rocks, near Cochití Pueblo, south of Santa Fe. At the base of the Jémez Mountains, the towering cone-shaped formations, some as tall as 90 feet, were formed over the past million years after a series of cataclysmic volcanic eruptions covered the area with hundreds of feet of ash, pumice and volcanic tuff. Gradually, wind and water eroded the softer material, leaving tent-shaped formations and narrow, winding canyons and sculpting the earth in contours and curves. Many of the cones are topped with boulders of harder rock, called cap rocks, which appear to be resting in precarious balance. Designated a national monument in 2001, the area's official name is Kasha-Katuwe Tent Rocks National Monument. The name means "white cliffs" in the Keresan language of the Cochití Pueblo people.

Joel took his camera there for the first time one summer morning and came back with material and inspiration that fueled a series of paintings for more than half a year. "The day I went, the clouds were billowing, thunder was rolling, eagles were screeching. I was pretty awestruck," he remembers. "There are all these strange, amazing shapes, these swirly shapes, which is what I'm interested in. You can let your imagination run wild." Which, of course, he did. The convex and concave movement of the land, scooped in and rounded out in curvilinear flow, provided him with the perfect components for exploring jazzy abstractions in compositional design.

The process was not without its challenges, though. "It's devilishly hard to paint because the colors are so subtle. You have to augment them, since it really is a gray and khaki place," Joel explains. Most of the hues he uses are, in fact, suggested in the land itself. They've merely been enhanced through the magic and creative freedom of art.

A hike among the looming, otherworldly Tent Rocks cones, especially in the intensity of an imminent storm, can border on the unnerving: "It's eroding while you're walking through there. You can hear the sand falling," Joel notes.

Yet, in a reflection of the artist's characteristic approach, his depictions of the place evoke a spirit of gentle buoyancy. Wildly dancing cloud shapes are echoed in the animated branches of trees and lines of the land. This ebullient sense, combined with clean lines and the complexity of abstract designs, is reflective of an artist with mastery of his medium who has accepted art history's invitation to play.

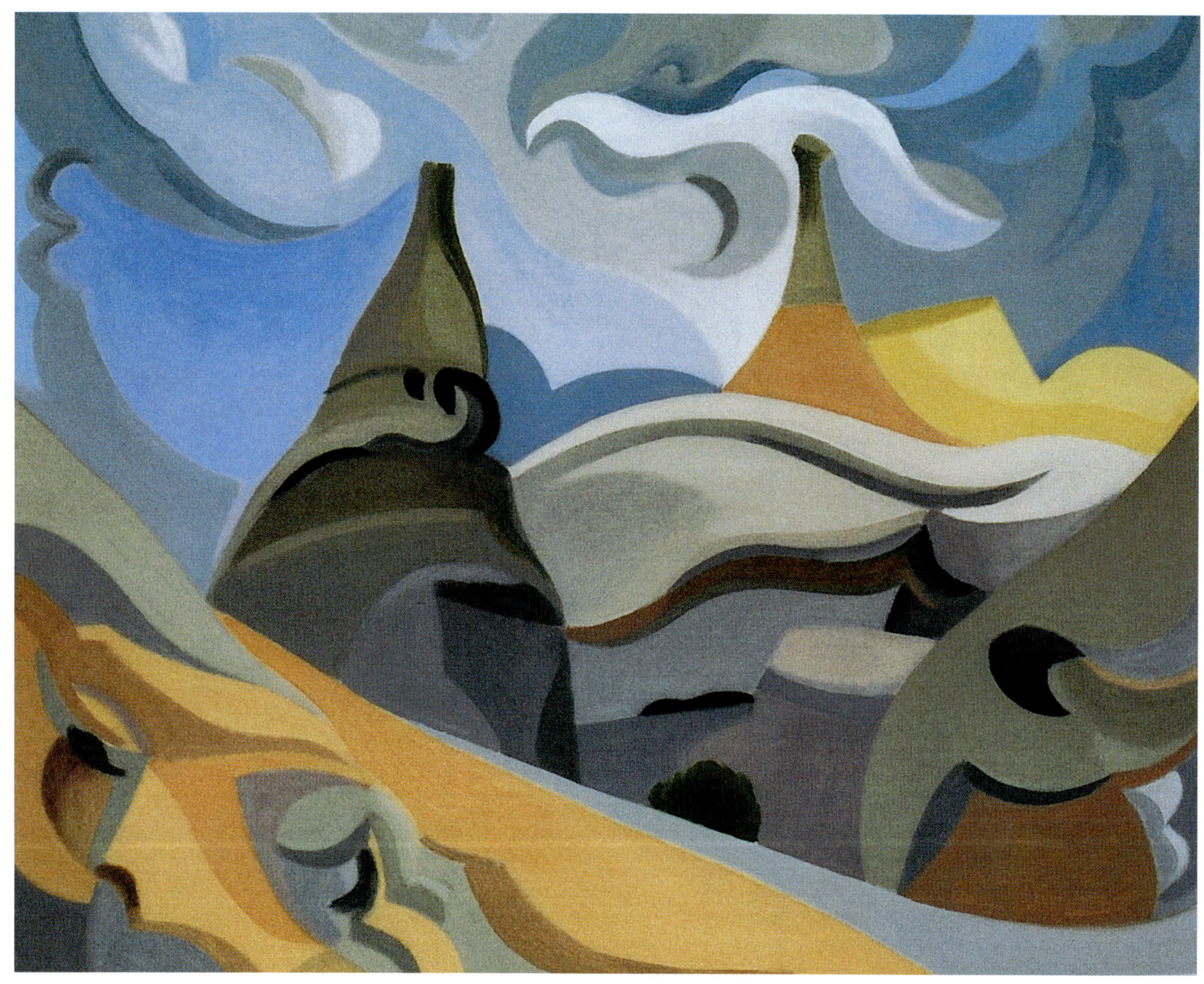

Tent Rocks, 2001 Oil on board, 14" × 18"

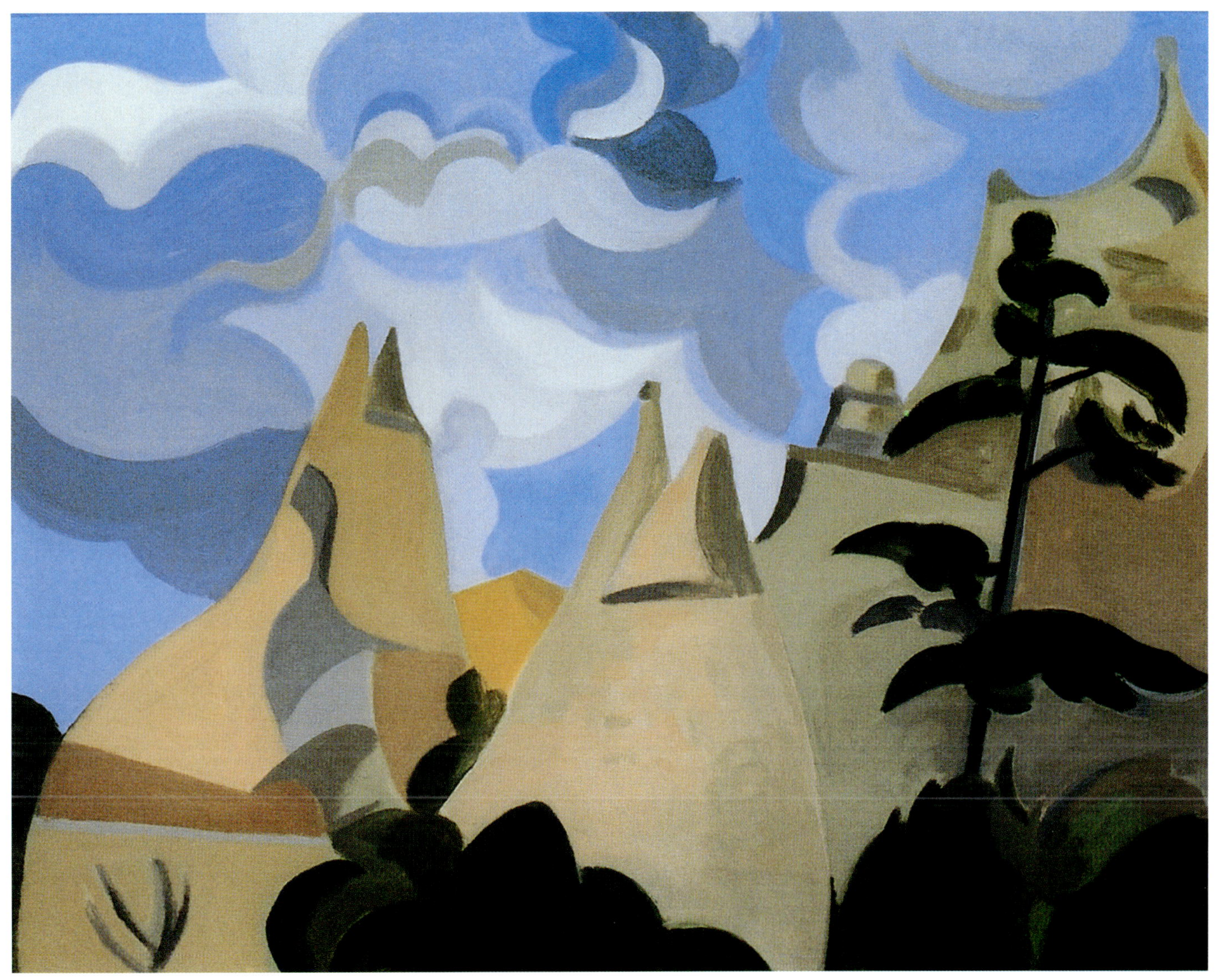

Tent Rocks, 2002

Oil on board, 11" × 14"

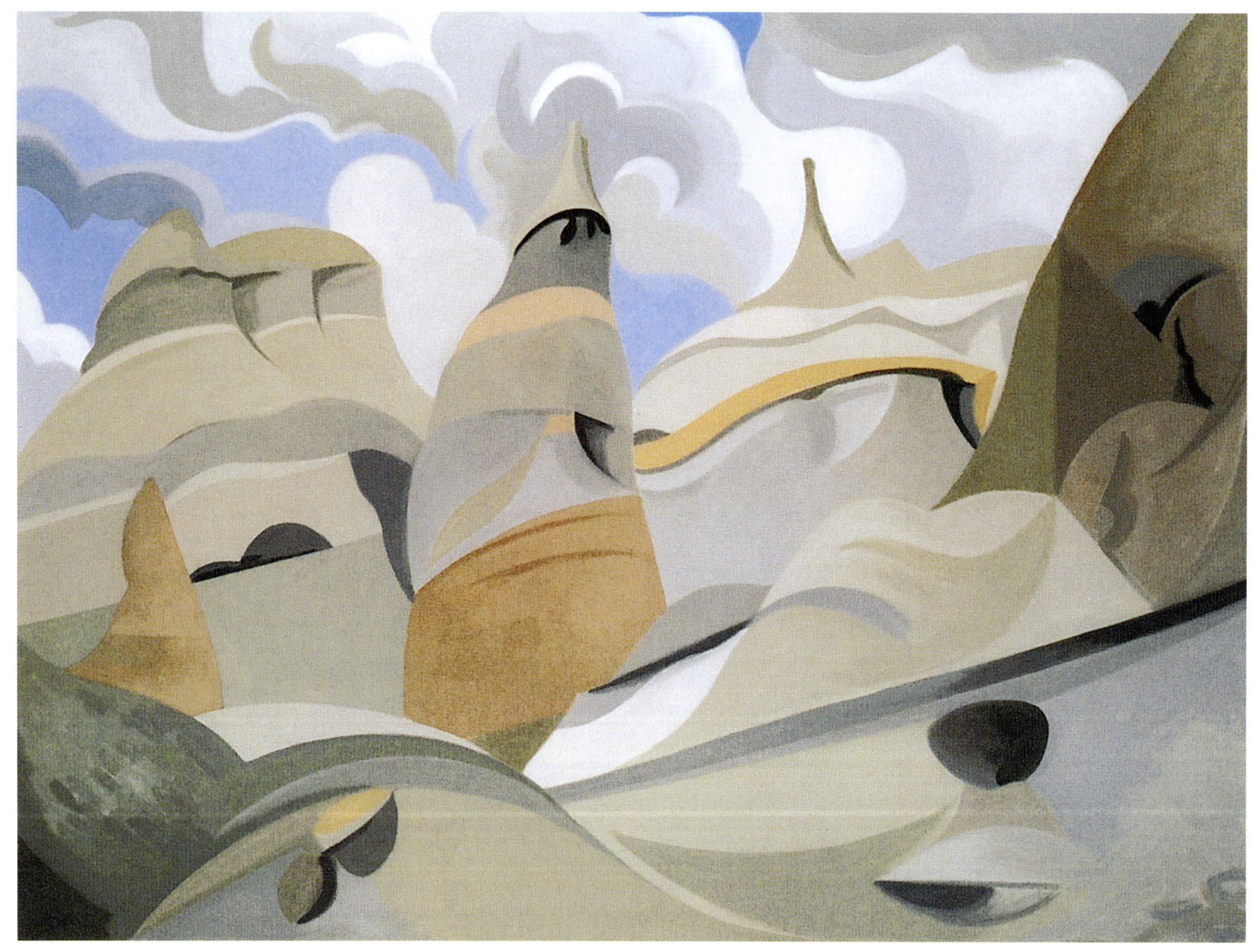

Tent Rocks, 2002 — Oil on linen, 22" × 30"

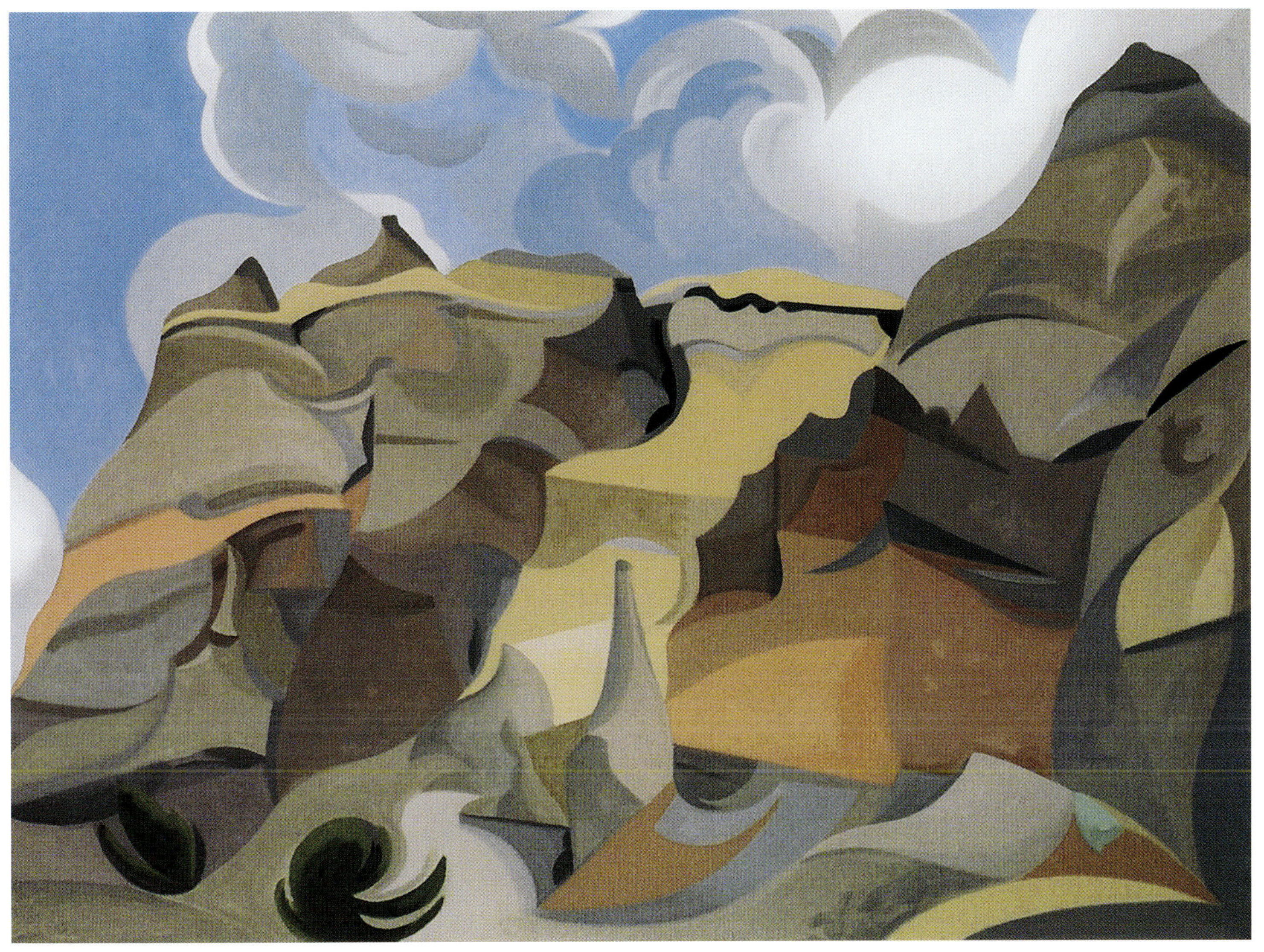

Tent Rocks, 2002 Oil on linen, 22" × 30"

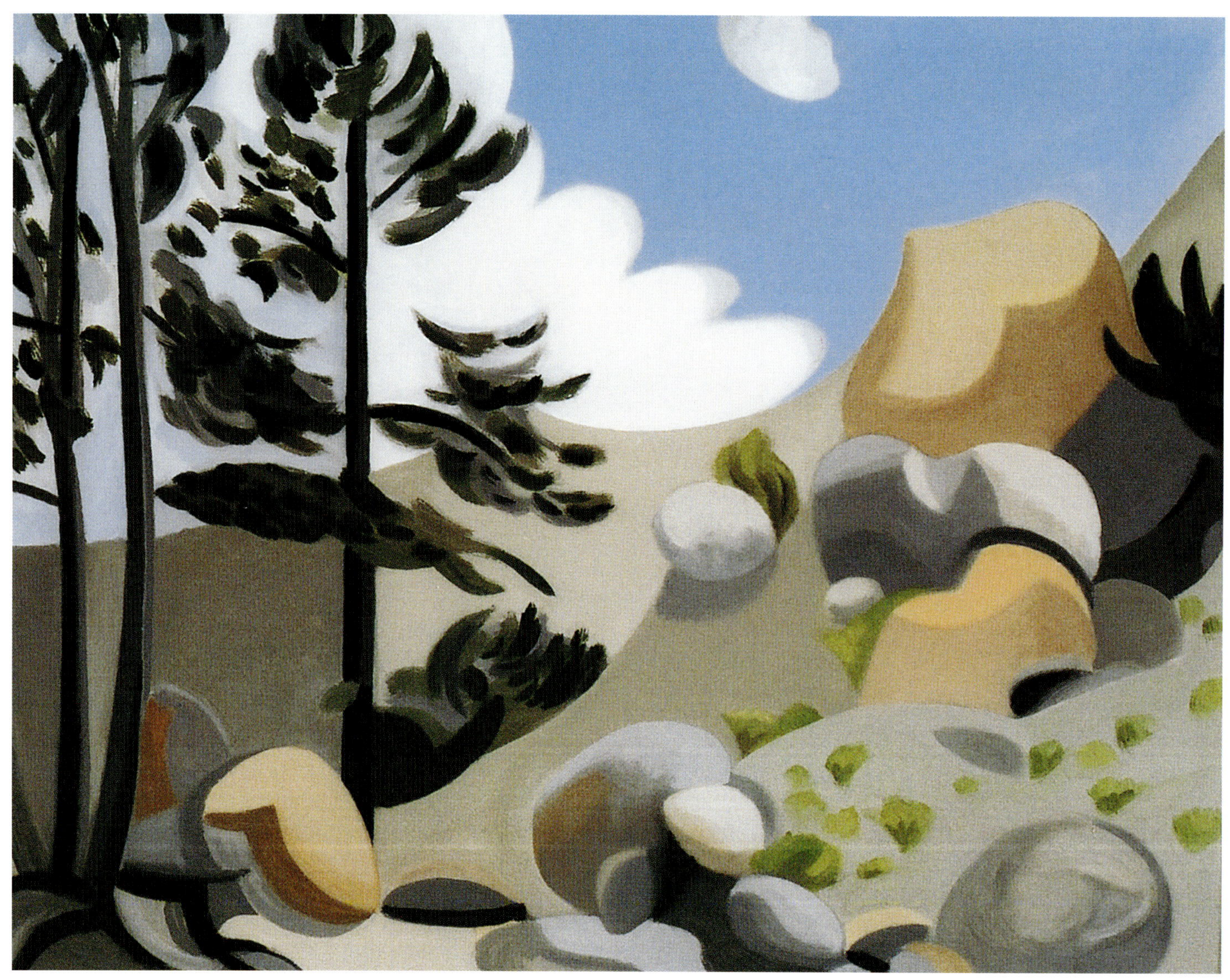

Rock Fall, Tent Rocks, 2003

Oil on board, 11" × 14"

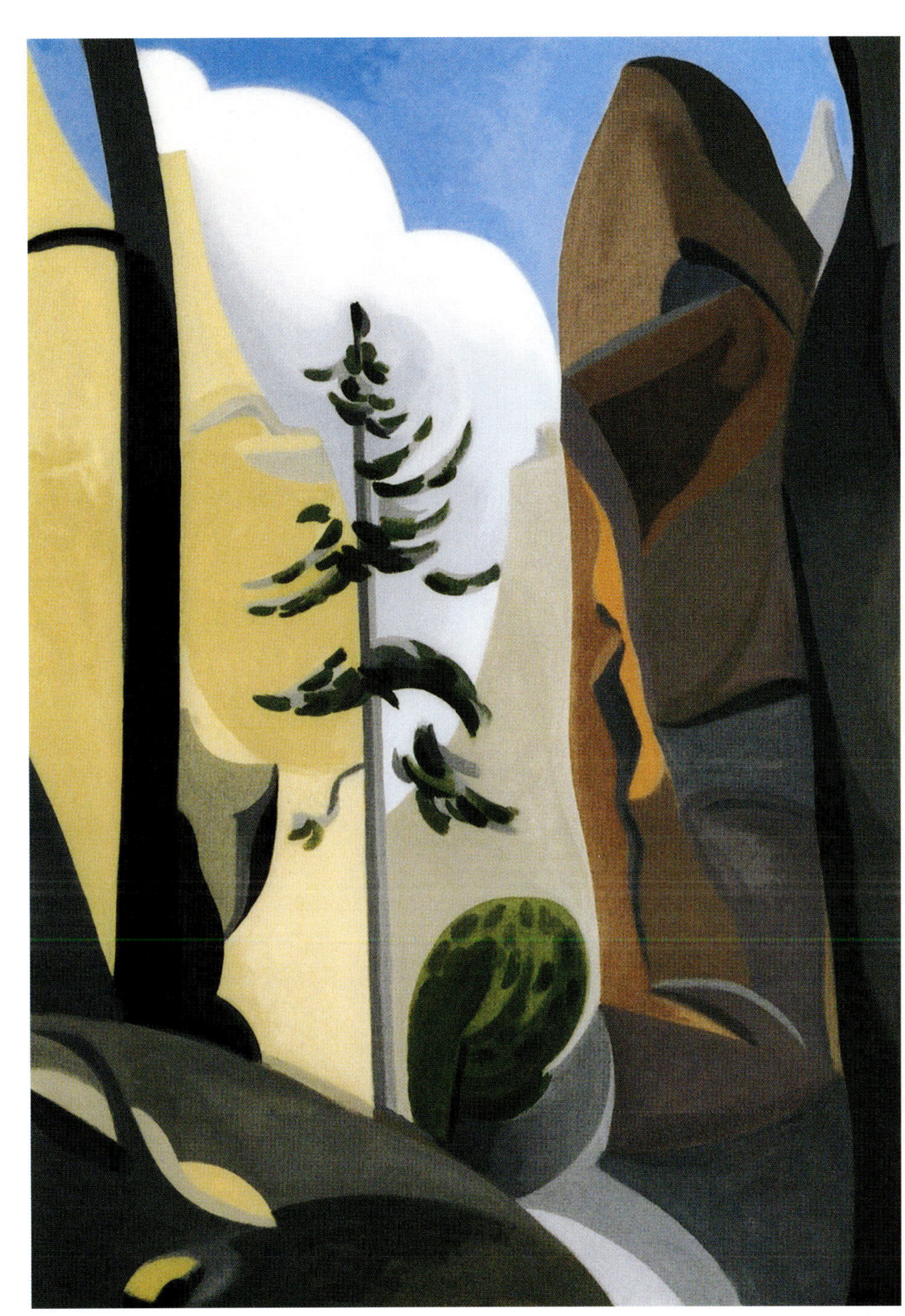

Tent Rocks, 2002
Oil on board, 24" × 17"

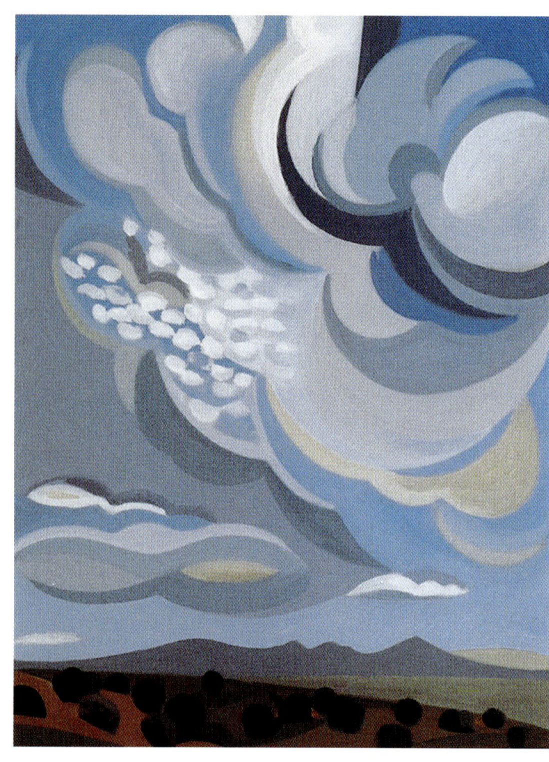

Clouds, 2002
Oil on board, 16" × 12"

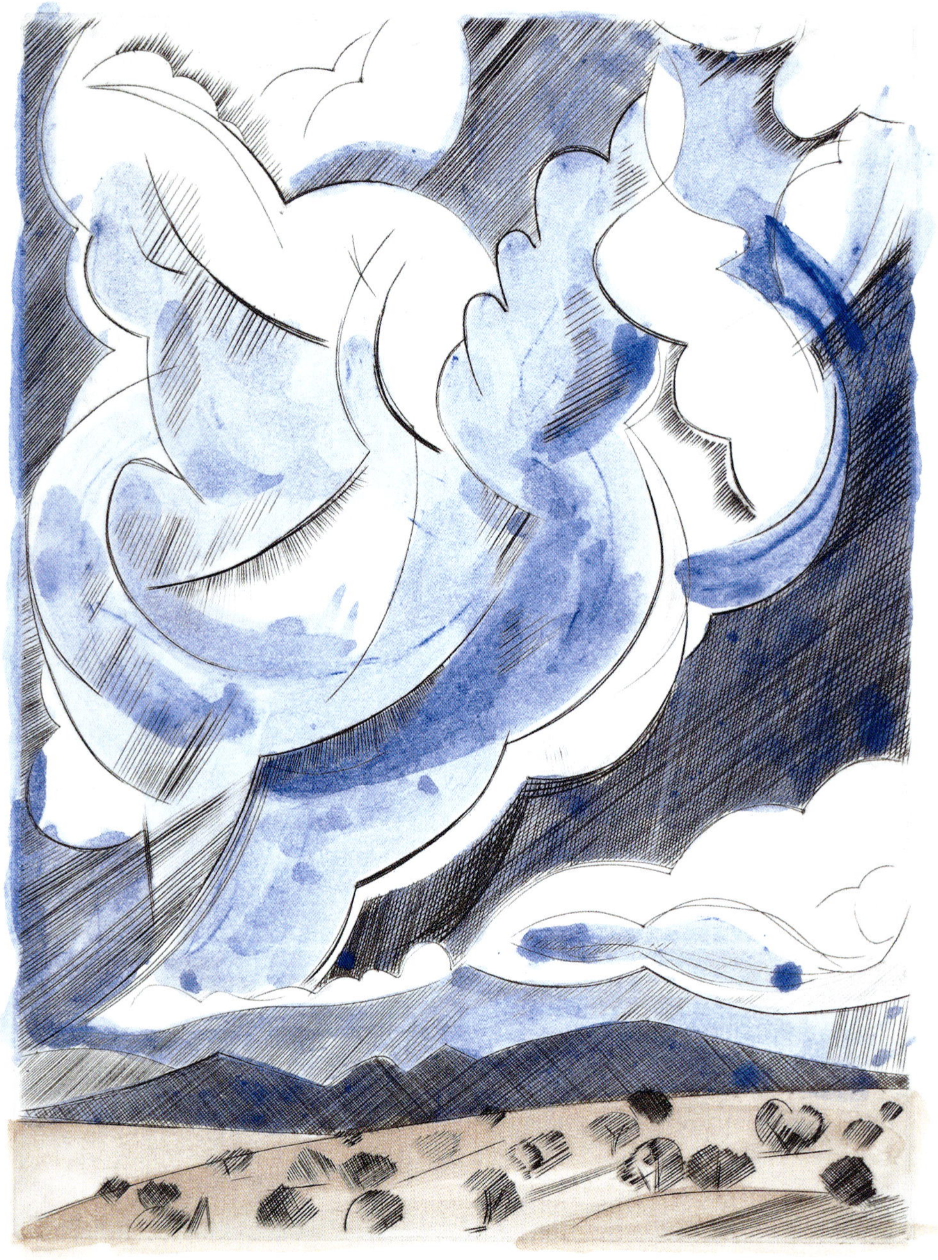

Study for *Clouds*, 2003
Hand-colored print, 7 ⅞" × 5 ⅞"

the printmaking process

Although experienced in a number of printmaking techniques, Joel often uses two major traditional intaglio methods, engraving and etching. Intaglio, from the Italian *intagliare*, means "to cut in, or engrave." For *Clouds*, the three-color print shown here, he used a combination of etching and engraving on copper plates. Zinc or brass plates sometimes are used with intaglio techniques, but copper is preferred for its optimum degree of hardness and evenness of grain.

The initial design for *Clouds* was inspired by an oil painting Joel previously had done. To re-create it as a print, he first cuts three copper plates of the same size. One will contain the black portions of the image, one the brown parts, and one the blue. As in all printmaking, the final print is the mirror image of the design produced on the plates.

For both the black and blue plates, Joel uses engraving. With a sharp tool called a burin, he carefully incises the image into the copper plates. Into one he cuts the lines that will hold black ink, and into the other plate goes the design to be printed in blue. With engraving, the burin's point is inserted into the copper and the tool is pushed forward, not with force but with finesse. For curved lines, the burin is held steady and pushed while the plate is turned.

To create the brown portion of *Clouds*—the low foreground hills—Joel prepares a third copper plate using the intaglio method known as etching. For this he covers the plate with an acid-resistant, waxy substance and then presses a fabric into the wax in the shape of the low hills. When the fabric is removed, the copper in that portion of the plate is partially exposed. Then he places the plate in an acid bath for a short time. The acid eats into, or etches, the copper in the shape of hills, leaving the rest of the plate blank. During the printing process, this etched area holds the ink and produces a soft, textured look, like the soft brown earth of the hills. In all, 30 to 40 hours of meticulous work goes into creating the three plates for *Clouds* before the printing process can begin.

Joel has two solid, well-built presses, the one used for *Clouds* dating from the 1920s. To begin printing, he heats the first copper plate and uses a roller to cover it with ink. He presses the ink into the plate with a dauber, making sure the ink fills all the lines of the design. Next, wiping the plate with a special cloth, he carefully removes ink from all but the incised lines and areas intended to hold color. This step may seem simple but is crucial to ensuring a clean final image, Joel explains.

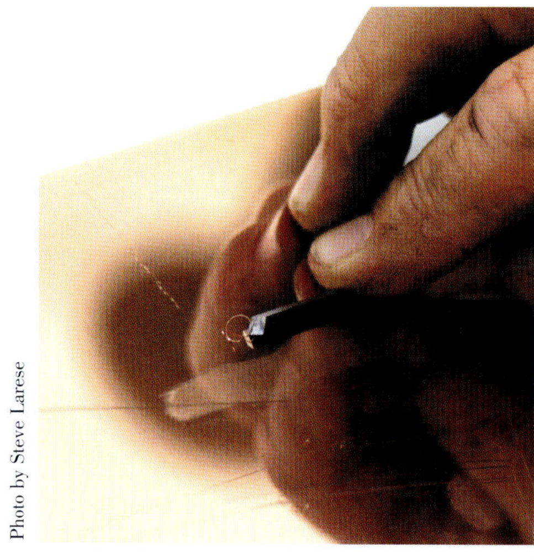
Photo by Steve Larese

Joel engraves the copper plate using the burin. This technique was used to engrave the lines of the design into the blue and black plates.

The design on the brown plate was etched into the copper plate using an acid bath.

brown plate

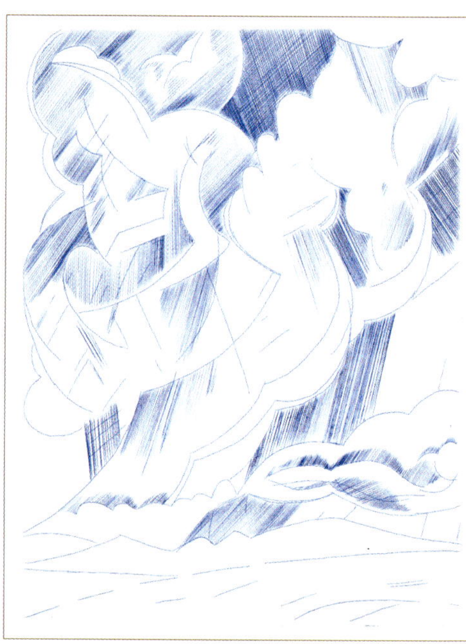
blue plate

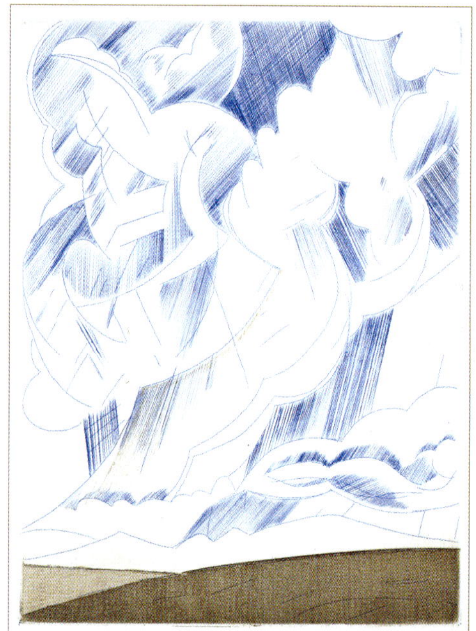
brown plate plus blue plate

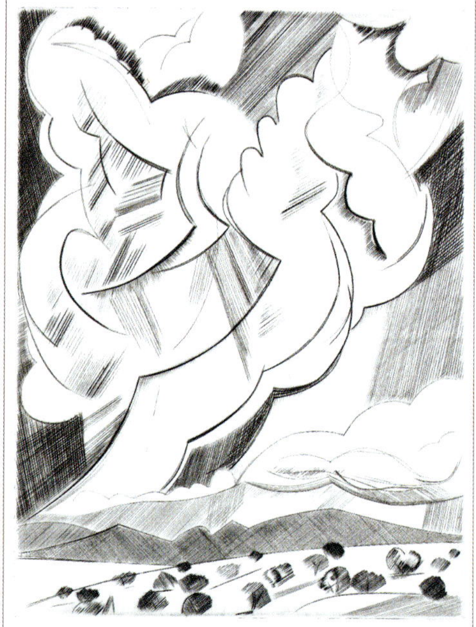
black plate

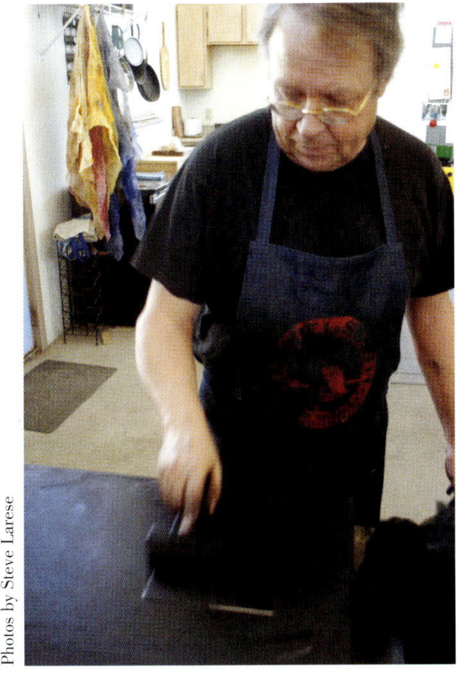

Photos by Steve Larese

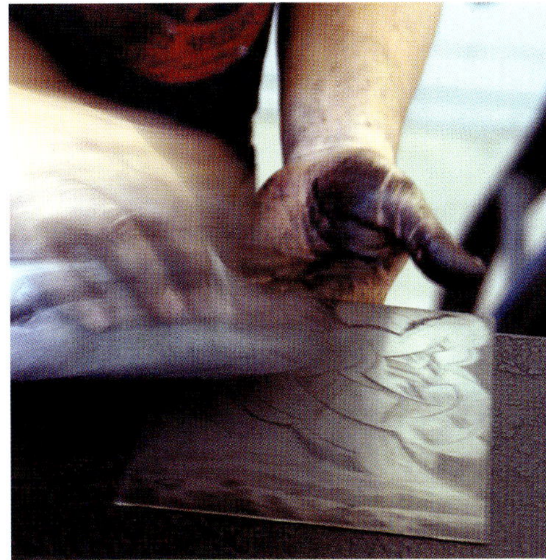

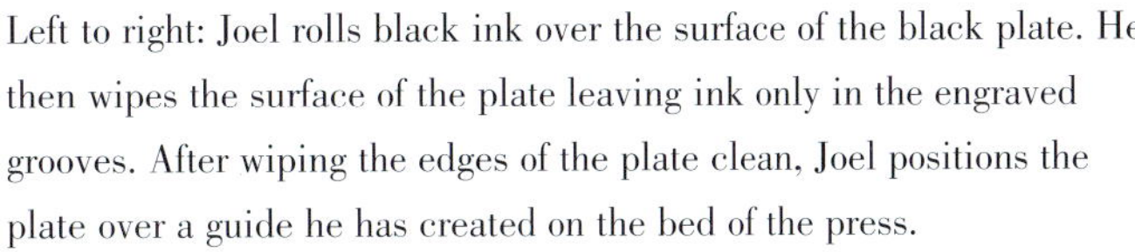

Left to right: Joel rolls black ink over the surface of the black plate. He then wipes the surface of the plate leaving ink only in the engraved grooves. After wiping the edges of the plate clean, Joel positions the plate over a guide he has created on the bed of the press.

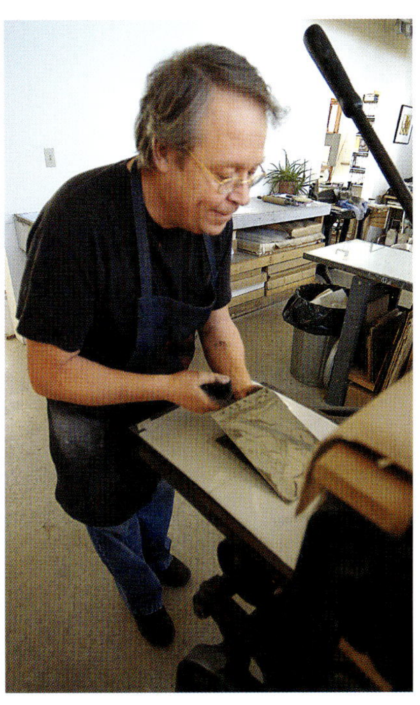

Now the copper plate is ready to go into the press. The paper to be printed on has been prepared by being soaked in water. The inked and wiped plate is placed on the press bed, face up, and one sheet of paper is placed over that. It is lined up so the image will be printed precisely in the right place on the paper. Then several layers of wool felt are laid on top of the paper to create the right amount of soft pressure between the paper and the heavy steel roller.

The wheel is turned—a feat that requires two hands and a strong back. The roller squeezes the plate against the paper, transferring the ink. Joel, often with the help of an assistant, will repeat the brown printing on as many sheets of paper as there will be prints in the edition. Then he will go through the same steps again, using blue ink on the second plate, and then again, with black ink on the third plate. For each print in the edition of *Clouds*, the paper has gone through the press three times, superimposing the three colors of the design to create a strong yet delicately subtle picture. The final step: the artist signs and numbers each print.

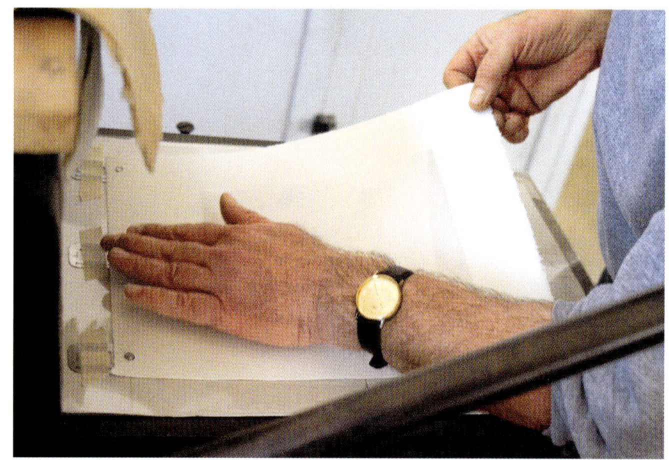

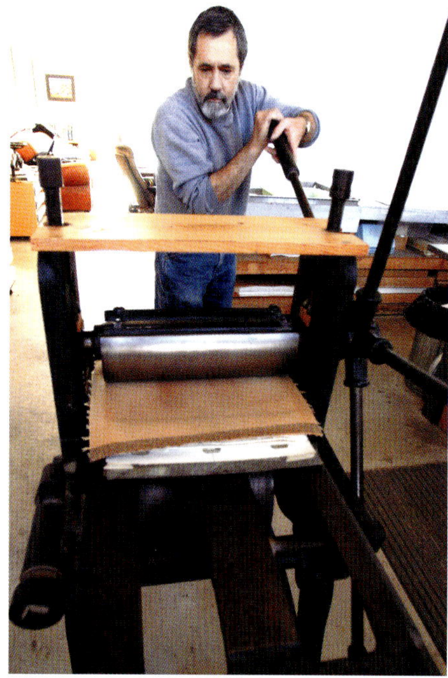

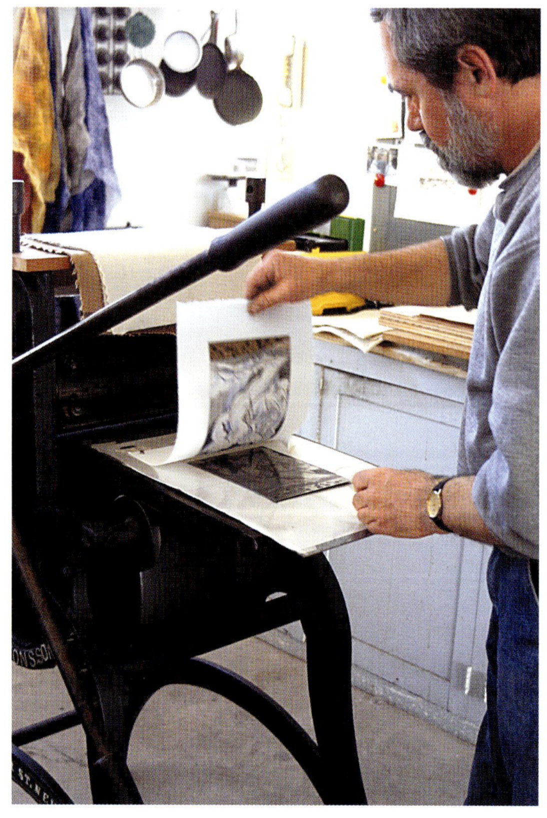

Clockwise from top left: Whitman Johnson, Joel's assistant on this project, carefully positions the sheet of paper on top of the plate on the bed of the press. The top of each sheet has been punched with holes that align on pins to assure that all 300 sheets will be in the same position as they go through the press.

The blanketed bed of the press is pulled under the press's roller.

Whitman pulls the sheet off the black plate to reveal the completed design, which is reproduced on the opposite page.

Clouds, 2003
Intaglio print, 7 ⅞" × 5 ⅞"

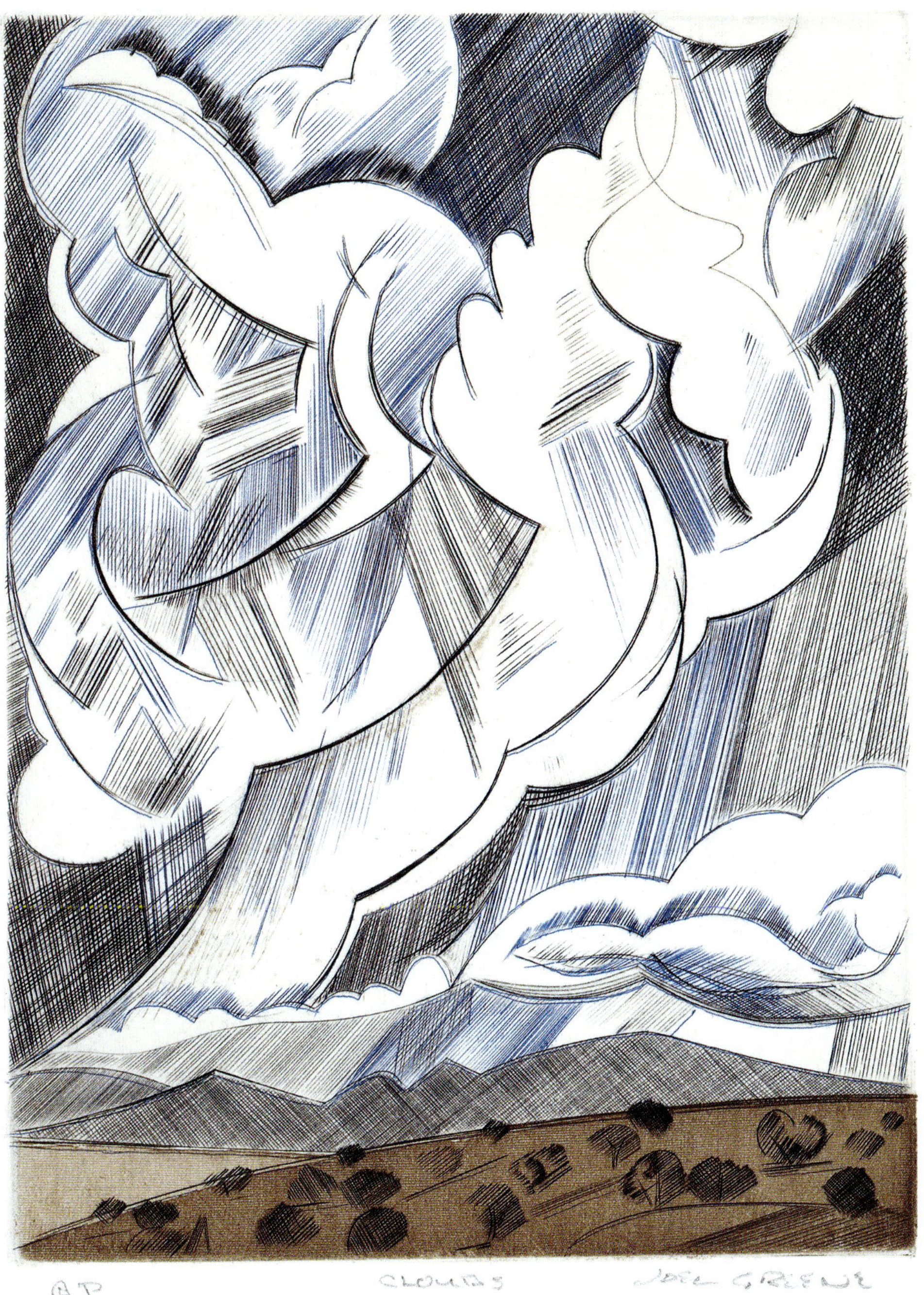

vita

Born

May 4, 1953, Denver, Colo.

Education

1966-1971, Robertson High School, Las Vegas, N.M.
1971-1975, B.F.A. University of Iowa, Iowa City, Iowa
1973, New Mexico Highlands University, Las Vegas, N.M.
1976-1978, M.A., University of Iowa, Iowa City, Iowa
1978-1981, M.F.A., University of Iowa, Iowa City, Iowa

Professional experience

1979-1981, research assistant, University of Iowa School of Art and Art History, Iowa City, Iowa
1982-1983, associate professor, drawing and printmaking, New Mexico Highlands University, Las Vegas, N.M.
1982, intaglio printmaking demonstration, Santa Fe Festival of the Arts, Santa Fe, N.M.
1984, demonstration, Making Printing Ink by Hand, Santa Fe Book Arts Festival, Museum of New Mexico, Palace of the Governors, Santa Fe, N.M.
1981-present, private print shop and intaglio workshop, private lessons in intaglio printmaking, Santa Fe, N.M.
1991, seminar, Options for Art Graduates, University of Iowa School of Art and Art History, Iowa City, Iowa
1983-present, full-time artist, painting and printmaking

Group and solo exhibitions

1979, Metropolitan Gallery, Cedar Falls, Iowa
1979, M.A. group exhibit, Eve Drewelowe Gallery, University of Iowa School of Art and Art History, Iowa City, Iowa
1980, Iowa Memorial Union, University of Iowa, Iowa City, Iowa
1980, Museum of Art, University of Iowa, Iowa City, Iowa
1982, Colorado Graphic Arts Center, Denver, Colo.
1983, Haven Restaurant, Santa Fe, N.M., intaglio prints
1984, Little Plaza Gallery, Santa Fe, N.M.

1985, 1986, Banquest Christmas Art Show, Banquest Central Offices, Santa Fe, N.M.
1987, Stables Art Center, Taos, N.M.
1988, Fox Fine Arts Center, University of Texas, El Paso, Texas
1990, The Bookroom and Coffee Bar, Santa Fe, N.M., etchings
2002, Foothills Art Center, Golden, Colo.
2003, Santa Fe Art Institute, printmaking show curated by Ron Adams, Santa Fe, N.M.
1982-present, Ernesto Mayans Gallery, Santa Fe, N.M., solo exhibitions

Museums, collections

Museum of New Mexico's Fine Arts Museum, Santa Fe, N.M.
Harwood Foundation, Taos, N.M.
Roswell Museum and Fine Art Center, Roswell, N.M.
University of New Mexico Museum, Albuquerque, N.M.
New Mexico Highlands University, Library Fine Arts Collection, Las Vegas, N.M.
Arizona State University Fine Arts Museum, Tempe, Ariz.
University of West Virginia Fine Arts Museum, Morgantown, W. Va.

Honors and distinctions

Theta Sigma, University of Iowa, 1975
Ford Foundation Scholarship, University of Iowa, 1976-1976
Research assistantship, University of Iowa School of Art and Art History, 1979-81
M.F.A. thesis, *Setting up and Maintaining an Intaglio Printshop*, 1981, in use for many years as shop handbook and valuable resource for art department and students, University of Iowa

Books

Joel Greene: Angles of Vision, by Robert Bell and James Mann (Bell Tower Editions, 2004), Santa Fe Printmakers Series

Gallery representation

Ernesto Mayans Gallery, Santa Fe, N.M.
sonya@mayansgallery.com

about the author

Santa Fe resident Gussie Fauntleroy has been writing about art and artists since 1986. She is the author of *Roxanne Swentzell: Extra Ordinary People*, published in 2001 as part of *New Mexico Magazine's* Artist Series. As a full-time freelance writer, she contributes monthly to *Southwest Art* and has written for a number of other national and regional magazines, including *Art & Antiques*, *New Mexico Magazine*, *Cowboys & Indians*, *The Santa Fean*, *Southern Accents* and *Native Peoples Magazine.* Her essays on artists have been published in museum and gallery exhibition catalogs. In addition, she is a book reviewer, occasional feature writer and weekly columnist for *The Santa Fe New Mexican, a* daily newspaper.

In 2003 Gussie was a guest commentator on a segment of National Public Radio's *Living on Earth*. Her commentary, excerpted from a thought-provoking essay first published in *Orion* magazine, was based on her experience of "life in a walk-in fridge," as she calls it: living for more than 10 years (comfortably, she contends, thanks to appropriate layers of clothing) in a house whose temperature in winter ranged between 45 and 55 degrees. Other notable life phases have included restoring and living in a 100-year-old chestnut log cabin in Virginia's Blue Ridge Mountains, selling solar heating systems in northern New Mexico and working for five years as a reporter in a dusty, south-central New Mexico cow town. She has lived in six states, as well as Canada, Japan and France. She has been married since 1979 to Dearing Fauntleroy, a homeopath, artist and musician.

When she began work on this book, Gussie discovered Joel was a neighbor of hers and that, aside from sharing a love of art, they have something else in common: they both drive Miata convertibles. His is white; hers is yellow with a red interior—the colors of the New Mexico flag.

Gussie can be contacted at faunt7@earthlink.net.

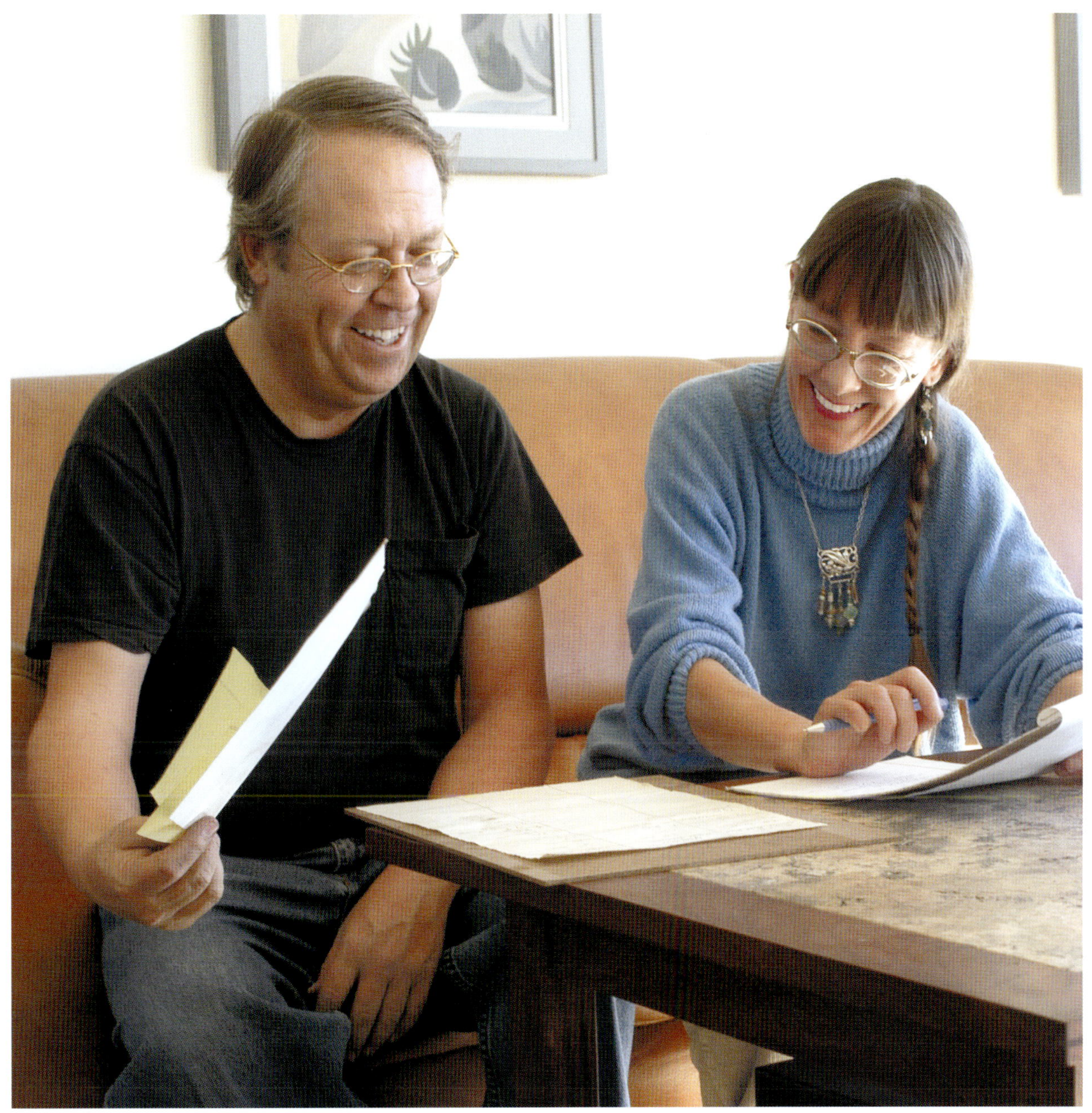

Joel Greene and Gussie Fauntleroy, 2004 Photo by Steve Larese

the new mexico magazine artist series

The Serigraphs of Doug West
Published in 1995
68 pages, 28 full-color reproductions

Howl: The Artwork of Luis Jimenez
Published in 1997
76 pages, 60 full-color reproductions

The Magical Realism of Alyce Frank
Published in 1999
96 pages, 43 full-color reproductions

Roxanne Swentzell, ExtraOrdinary People
Published in 2003
96 pages, 85 full-color reproductions